Between Justice & Mercy

with

Related Essays

Ron Smith, MD

[11] For I know the plans I have for you, declares the LORD, plans for welfare and not for evil, to give you a future and a hope. [12] Then you will call upon me and come and pray to me, and I will hear you.

(Jer. 29:11–12 ESV)

WESTBOW
PRESS®
A DIVISION OF THOMAS NELSON
& ZONDERVAN

WestBow Press books may be ordered through booksellers or by contacting:

WestBow Press
A Division of Thomas Nelson & Zondervan
1663 Liberty Drive
Bloomington, IN 47403
www.westbowpress.com
844-714-3454

ISBN: 978-1-6642-2011-9 (sc)
ISBN: 978-1-6642-2012-6 (e)

Print information available on the last page.

WestBow Press rev. date: 01/14/2021

To my Stacy

[1] The Song of Songs, which is Solomon's.
[2] Let him kiss me with the kisses of
his mouth!
For your love is better than wine;
[3] your anointing oils are fragrant;
your name is oil poured out;
therefore virgins love you.
[4] Draw me after you; let us run.
The king has brought me into his
chambers.
We will exult and rejoice in you; we
will extol your love more than
wine; rightly do they love you.

Song of Solomon 1:1-4 ESV

Table of Contents

I. Between Justice and Mercy

II. Essays

Foreword

To grasp and experience God's justice and mercy and understand what is between the two, one first must accept the fact that God is sovereign.

Ronnie Smith explores the benevolent aspects of God's sovereign mercy and grace. He believes God's love does not demand something in return from his creation. He allows his creation to decide to respond to his love—and return love, trust, and obedience. This begs the question: can a rejected sovereign really continue to bestow mercy, grace love on those who reject him? Smith's answer to the question is yes, but often the justice, mercy and love do not come in the form we desire or expect.

Smith briefly works through an accepted truth: there are certain codes for behavior (rules, laws, etc.) which everyone is expected and required to adhere. Governments, kings, and sovereigns all have them. Violation of those codes of behavior requires justice. Justice—a penalty or price to make or erase the violation as if it had not happened—is set by the offended. Smith gives Bona Fides to God that he is the offended and humanity is the offender. We owe something to God.

Humanity has violated (and still does) God's laws. Even though God loves us expecting nothing in return, a violated law still requires justice. There is a price to pay. Thus argues Smith, God cannot be a just God without requiring justice. We owe something to God, but what? Scripture tells us the required price, and that makes us turn to him and cry, "Mercy!"

Mercy doesn't mean there is an easy fix. Mercy from a sovereign God still requires justice and payment.

Yet Smith explains that. God's love for us reverses the order of justice and mercy. Rather than us paying the price, he satisfied his own justice with the life of his son Jesus. His life, teaching, death and resurrection reach between mercy and justice. He proves he will give everything he has for us.

In the first Passover, justice and mercy were both served. The blood of a lamb spared the Hebrews in Egypt. The blood of the LAMB, Jesus, spared Christians' lives in the Second Passover.

Ronnie's research of the Second Passover details the timeline of Jesus's life. It dives deep into his teaching about the Old Testament prophetic fulfillment, identity, and purpose of the Messiah. This book explains how Jesus bridges judgment and mercy.

Knowing Ronnie Smith as I do, his genuine faith in Jesus Christ, his love for God, his search for Biblical truth and his desire to share those truths, I highly recommend this book. I may have repeated myself several times, but he has satisfied the title of his book. I highly recommend it to you.

—Thomas W. Langford, Sr., Retired Pastor, AA, BA, Mdiv, September 28, 2020

Editor's Note

I appreciate Dr. Ron Smith's intensive research to address a couple of "stumbling blocks" that have arisen for those examining the Christian faith. First, as depicted in his title, *Between Justice and Mercy*, is the erroneous dichotomy of the God of the Old Testament versus the God of the New Testament. Many get caught up in seeing God as a wrathful, Zeus-like god in the sky, ready to strike us down. But Dr. Smith goes to great lengths to show that God's mercy is and always has been present, even from humanity's first act of disobedience.

The other difficulty for a thinking person is reconciling the three days in the tomb that Jesus himself predicted with the "Good Friday" scenario most widely taught. I commend Dr. Ron for digging deep into the Hebrew calendar and culture of the time to help those unfamiliar with these to see the timeline from the right perspective. He carefully constructs a thorough argument for the crucifixion happening on Wednesday so that a full three days in the tomb take place, then—glory to God—Christ the FirstFruits offering arose on the first day of the week.

—Shauna Perez, editor and fellow student of the Word for twenty-seven years, September 22, 2020

Preface

We relate to God unconsciously in one of two ways. He is either primarily sovereign, or he is loving. We rarely combine them, but easily confuse them.

It is almost uncanny how often that the phrase "sovereign God" ranks above "loving God." We use the first phrase when we want to project his power and the second when we want to project his compassion. The phrase "loving God," to us, does not carry the necessary solemnness as the other. It gets short shrift. How we speak about and to him, using these two, reveals the depth of our relationship with him.

You may be a believer or a skeptic with serious questions. Is there really a God? Did creation just happen from a cosmic roll of the dice? Is God always good? Everyone needs to know the answers to those questions, because they are necessary to grasp the connection between justice and mercy. That requires we understand what sovereignty and love are, and the difference between them.

Though God can arrange circumstances conducive to improving us, his sovereignty cannot save anyone. Only when we come face to face with the *loving, merciful* God can we be made whole. Without question, God *is* sovereign—but he does not call us *subjects*.

He calls us *children*.

PART I

BETWEEN JUSTICE AND MERCY

CHAPTER ONE

Sovereignty or Love

A defendant needs a judge with impeccable character who renders fair verdicts. This makes an understanding of God's character essential, because he is *the* fair and just judge of all the world.

Attributes are dimensions or ranges of authority and effect. All earthly judges have jurisdictions, i.e., dimensions, where their judgments apply. The quality of their verdicts pin them as a "good" or "bad" judge, but jurisdiction has no effect on outcome. Sentencing is where a judge's character becomes significant.

Unlike an earthly judge, God's justice and mercy stem entirely from his character. However, the dimensions of his jurisdiction do not define the quality of his verdicts or appropriateness of his sentences. We commonly confuse God's character with his attributes, but they are not the same. Who God is, comes down to his core character trait. His attributes define *where* that character has effect.

Attributes or Character. Over the centuries, each sovereign of Great Britain has had an official style of address. We formally address the current Queen of England as follows.

> Elizabeth II, by the Grace of God of the United Kingdom of Great Britain and Northern Ireland and of her other Realms and Territories Queen, Head of the Commonwealth, Defender of the Faith

Notice that sovereignty describes her range or boundary of authority. Though she cannot be everywhere at once in her sovereign domain, her subjects sense her presence through the agencies of government, i.e., police, public servants, and military authorities. These official agents represent her and relay the state of her realm. Substantial though her power may be, she is not all-powerful. The boundary of her realm constrains the reach of her power.

In themselves, her ruling dimensions say nothing about what the Queen of England is like. Sovereignty is unrelated to her character and gives no insight into it. Only the way she Acts after she becomes the sovereign reveals her character.

Sovereignty qualifies character through the lens of public perception, which plays some part in defining it. Our understanding of sovereignty from earthly sovereigns does not apply to God. Public perception does not change him the way it can change earthly rulers.

Historical Sovereignty. Each British monarch over the centuries shaped their public impression. Their Acts stemmed from their character and defined anew the public perception of what the term sovereign meant to their subjects. People of today can look back at monarchs in bygone eras and more easily see how each spun a distinct flavor of how people thought about sovereignty.

Sovereign monarchs such as Queen Anne (1665–1714), Henry VIII (1491–1547), and Queen Victoria (1837–1901) formed varied impressions of the term sovereignty. Each of them added to or changed what the term sovereign meant to their subjects. English monarchs were sometimes ruthless and despised, while a few were decent, revered, and even adored.

Henry VIII, who was king from 1509 to 1547, disposed himself of five of his six wives, and so changed the English constitution by employing the theory of the divine right of kings. Queen Anne, who ruled from 1707 to 1714, killed her elder sister Mary, Queen of Scots in a sordid script. Edward VIII, who reigned for less than the full year of 1936, abdicated because he could not take his chosen wife to be Queen. George VI succeeded his disgraced brother and reigned for the rest of 1936 until early 1952. From all accounts, his subjects thought fondly of him while many despised Edward.

Who can forget the royal mess after Prince Charles, the future King of England, divorced Princess Diana? When Queen Elizabeth II remained aloof about Diana, it left another indelible stain on the word sovereign. Will anyone consider Prince Charles's behavior if and when he ascends the throne? Probably they will not.

Over the years, the sovereign throne of Great Britain has taken a beating, but not so much because people want to eliminate it. With each monarch, sovereignty slowly became unbound from character. Now to *be* the sovereign means you can do just about whatever you want, because sovereignty is higher than character. As my Jewish friend and guide in Israel repeatedly said, "It is good to be the king."

Boundless Morality. Does the term sovereign really imply that the bearer's actions are unassailable? Can a sovereign person behave any way they want without fear of moral critique? A quick dictionary review from the Apple® Dictionary app of the word sovereign supports that notion.

> **sov·er·eign** | ˈsäv(ə)rən |
> **noun**
> **1** a supreme ruler, especially a monarch: the Emperor became the first Japanese sovereign to visit Britain.
> **adjective**
> possessing supreme or ultimate power: in modern democracies the people's will is in theory sovereign.
> • [attributive] archaic or literary possessing royal power and status: our most sovereign lord the King.

Notice that no part of the definition implies anything about character or morality. As I demonstrated, this *is* the public perception that sovereignty defines morality. Many think the sovereign God is like that and can do anything he wants. Does God's boundless sovereignty supersede moral rightness and character?

⌗

The Sovereignty of God. Understanding how we think of phrases like "sovereign king" is important because we apply the same reasoning to the phrase "sovereign God." Earthly sovereigns seem to easily get a pass for offenses ranging from minor infractions to serious misconduct. Sovereignty sets character aside and even gives license for bad behavior. After all, it is good to be the king.

God gets no such pass. Every time the next terrorist catastrophe occurs or one of our desperate prayers goes unanswered, God is easily targeted. Consider this excerpt from C. S. Lewis's *The Problem of Pain.*[1]

> "If God were good, He would wish to make His creatures perfectly happy, and if God were almighty, He would be able to do what He wished. But the creatures are not happy. Therefore, God lacks either goodness, or power, or both." This is the problem of pain, in its simplest form.

This embodies exactly my point. It assumes that because God is all-powerful, he can and should fix everything. His character means nothing. Is moral character second to sovereign power for God the way it is for earthly sovereigns? What defines God—his sovereignty or his character?

God's boundless sovereignty, power, presence, and knowledge *cannot* overrule his character. His character defines him, and he *will not* act outside of it for any reason. That means there are things he cannot do. God is not weak, rather this is why we call him holy. His holiness streams from his character, not his sovereignty. We trust him because he is good and not because he is powerful.

God's boundless sovereign dimensions can never taint his character. His goodness does not exist because he is supremely sovereign. Attributes like omniscience, omnipotence, and omnipresence, etc., *never* dictate or guide his character.

---

[1] C. S. Lewis, *The Problem of Pain.*

The Center of God's Character. God's whole character comes from his core trait of agapē (Greek for agape, ag-ah´-pay) love. The King James Bible calls it "charity," but the same Greek word is "love" in recent translations. One should not confuse the modern understanding of charity for its original meaning in the King James Bible. Notice the archaic dictionary definition, again from the Apple® Dictionary App, of the word below.

> **char·i·ty** | 'CHerədē |
> noun (plural **charities**)
> • **archaic** love of humankind, typically in a Christian context: faith, hope, and charity.

I like this description in Moody's Bible Commentary.

> Love is "a spontaneous inward affection of one person for another that manifests itself in an outgoing concern for the other and impels one to self-giving."[2]

God's love differs from *storge, philia,* and *eros,* the other kinds which Lewis described in *The Four Loves.* His love is selfless and gives itself, requiring nothing in return. What he gives, however, is not a thing but *himself.* What Jesus Christ promised the thief on the cross was not paradise—it was paradise *with* him.

We should love God, not because we want to go to heaven or escape hell. Heaven is just the place where *he* is. He is the prize!

---

[2] Joseph A. Fitzmyer, *First Corinthians. A New Translation With Introduction and Commentary,* 32:489.

The Circle of Love. 1 Corinthians 13 concisely describes God's character. The Circle of Love above graphically illustrates this. Notice that *the* central characteristic is agape love. All of God's other character traits stream from his love. They each depend on his core trait of love. Agape love interacts differently with its object in contrast to *philia, storge*, and *eros*.

Storge is the love that a parent has for a child. *Philia* is the love that one friend has for another. *Eros* is the romantic love that a husband and wife have for each other. These types of love are fraught with reciprocal expectations, while agape love requires none. If we spurn the parent, friend, or lover, those relationships can suffer and die. If we spurn God and separate ourselves from him, his love remains.

Each characteristic on the circle also links to the one or more of the others. Justice and mercy require something more, however. How can such polar opposites as justice and mercy ever connect? Psalm 85:10 in both the Amplified and English Standard Version support their connection.

> [10] Mercy and loving-kindness and truth have met together; righteousness and peace have kissed each other. (Ps. 85:10 AMP)

¹⁰ Steadfast love and faithfulness meet; righteousness and peace kiss each other. (Ps. 85:10 ESV)

The Hebrew word צֶדֶק (*ṣedeq,* tseh´-dek) means righteousness, justice, rightness, acting according to a proper (God's) standard, doing what is right, and being in the right. The Hebrew word שָׁלוֹם (*šālom,* shaw-lome´) means peace, safety, prosperity, well-being; intactness, wholeness. Peace can have a focus of security, safety which can bring feelings of satisfaction, well-being, and contentment. Steadfast love comes from חֶסֶד (*hesed,* kheh´-sed) and means unfailing love, loyal love, devotion, kindness, often based on a prior relationship, and especially a covenant relationship.

God's agape love requires justice for the one who is wronged. It also requires mercy be offered for the transgressor. How can that be if we are at the same time both transgressor and victim? C. S. Lewis states God's position well.

> He [God] unhesitatingly behaved as if he was the party chiefly concerned, the person chiefly offended in all offences.³

Jesus's disciples, challenged with this conundrum, asked him, "Who then can be saved?" He replied, "With man this is impossible, but with God all things are possible." The story of Abraham and Isaac reveals the answer. As Isaac was preparing the altar, he asked Abraham where was the sacrifice. Abraham replied prophetically.

> ⁸ And Abraham said, My son, God will provide <u>himself</u> a lamb for a burnt offering: so they went both of them together. (Gen. 22:8 KJV)

Even then God tells us he *himself* can pay our price that his justice requires. The judge declares the sentence and then steps in to take the punishment, which is death. Why would God do this? His love for us is what motivates him. Sovereignty has nothing to do with it.

Consider why God's logic works. If we died to satisfy his justice, we remain dead and separated from him. We, the objects of his love, would be lost.

---

³ C. S. Lewis, *Mere Christianity.*

However, if he dies in our place, *he satisfies his own justice, restores mankind, and can live again* to be forever with us. Paradoxically, his death is the only way to bring life.

God lives and dies as a man, and mercy kisses justice.

CHAPTER TWO

What Was God Thinking

Did God create everything just because he could? Was creation ever intended to meet one of his needs? What would creation be like if he was evil and not good?

White and Black. Consider again this quotation from Lewis. From the implied assumption, God either fully controls his creation or he controls nothing.

> "If God were good, He would wish to make His creatures perfectly happy, and if God were almighty, He would be able to do what He wished. But the creatures are not happy. Therefore, God lacks either goodness, or power, or both." This is the problem of pain, in its simplest form.

The quote also assumes God's unbounded sovereignty and power gives him every right to manipulate every aspect of his creation. Yet, his character restrains him. God cannot do everything or even anything in particular just because he is supremely sovereign and all powerful.

We know he cannot lie. Scripture says so. Were that not a fact, justice would be void, and mercy becomes arbitrary. Truth must *always* be present in everything God does, and truth is derived from his core character of love.

> [17] Wherein God, willing more abundantly to shew unto the heirs of promise the immutability of his counsel, confirmed it by an oath: [18] That by two immutable things, in which it was impossible for God to lie, we might have a strong consolation, who have fled for refuge to lay hold

upon the hope set before us: [19] Which hope we have as an anchor of the soul, both sure and stedfast, and which entereth into that within the veil. (Heb. 6:17–19 KJV)

God's outer and core character traits stand or fall together. If one fails, then they all do. Good is all or nothing. Consider these two overlapping circles, one filled with white and the other black. The one on the left represents God's goodness. The one on the right represents evil, i.e., the complete lack of goodness. The circles overlap, but do not intersect. Like oil and water they cannot mix.

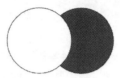

Suppose for argument there could be an intersection. Suppose that God was only partly good, and sometimes he was evil. Those circles might look something like this instead.

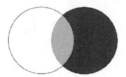

Where are the boundaries of God's goodness if part of him is good and part of him bad? Indeed, the intersection of the white and dark in the circles would not be partly white, partly gray, and partly black. Everything would be gray, as if you poured black and white paint together in a third can. This is what Scripture means when it says a little leaven leavens the whole lump of bread dough in both 1 Corinthians 5:6 and Galations 5:9.

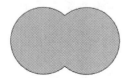

God is perfectly good, or he is not God at all. He would be nothing but a devilish demoniac. He would have no reason to create us with even a minuscule understanding of good and evil. He could not even know that he was evil. We would be slaves and not sons. Without question, evil is the absence of God's goodness, just as darkness is the absence of light. Evil and darkness are not perceivable without goodness and light.

Understanding what good and evil are proves that a good God exists. Perceiving goodness cannot result from any biologic process. All the other creatures are not inherently good or evil simply because they are biologically alive. They can be conditioned for a prescribed behavior, however they have no innate moral law and are not responsible for their actions as men and angels are.

Every time we say, "that isn't fair," or, "that's wrong," it proves we have an inner moral compass. God made us with the ability to know good and evil—we are made in his image. A moral scale hangs from our heart, and on it we weigh *everything* we think about. Sometimes we choose rightly and other times we do evil. Just knowing what good and evil are does not mean we are evil. Just because a good God knows all things, beginning to end, does not make him responsible for the bad things that happen.

C. S. Lewis called this the Law of Human Nature, the moral law. In that way, we are unique among all earthly creatures.

✢

Why God Creates. We know God is good, all-powerful, and without authoritative boundary. Only his unselfish love explains why he wanted to create anything. He didn't make us because *he* needs something from us; he needs nothing. Slaves exist for their master's use. Why would a supreme being *need* a slave for anything?

Our present moral mess proves, at least in our eyes, we would not be worth creating. Even the devil would take no pleasure in creatures that were all bad.

He certainly takes no interest in the third of the fallen angels who became the demons. Were we depraved and lost beyond God's reach, Satan would take no more notice of us than he does them. Remember, Satan is evil. Even if he had creative power, he *could not* create any good thing. His only motivation is to destroy any good he finds.

Only a good God can create good things and make man aware of the difference between good and evil. Only he would strive to know us and never abuse us. Only a loving God would want us. If he is a good God, then we are not slaves and puppets. His love *ensures* we are not abused or misused by him.

There are only two logical, mutually exclusive options. Either we are mindless subjects unaware of love, good, evil, right, wrong, and pain or pleasure, or God created us to know and experience a loving relationship with him. Since the first option is unequivocally impossible, we know we are loved, and loved greatly.

How God Creates. I love this excerpt from *The Last Battle* by C. S. Lewis. The dwarves find themselves in a dark, dirty stable, so they think. They choose not to see the great lion Aslan who has the power to save them.

> "You see," said Aslan. "They will not let us help them. They have chosen cunning instead of belief. Their prison is only in their own minds, yet they are in that prison; and so afraid of being taken in that they cannot be taken out."

This scene illustrates the most mysterious aspect of man's creation. I've shown you that God created us to fellowship with and love him. So how can a loving God create us without *making* each person love him? Either we are slaves and are being forced to "love" him, or we make our own independent choice. I've proven to you we are not slaves, so God necessarily cannot pre-program us to love him at the point he calls us into being.

Could he simply decide whether each created person had a true, bona fide choice by rolling the dice each time? Is the most important decision of our life just chance? Of course not. I've already shown you how his love prevents him from doing that.

When he tells Abram that his name is "I AM," he was not being clever. He was declaring his timelessness. God does not ride along on the stream of our time as we experience it. He does not rewind or fast forward the recording of our life to see what we do. There is no *before* or *after* for him. He sees all of our time as *now*. He knows *everything* that we will do or experience the instant he makes us.

So how can an all-knowing God create a unique person *without* making all their choices? This mystery reveals an amazing fact about God. He must choose *not* to know what choices we make before he creates us. But how can God do that? He *knows* everything. Can he who knows everything choose to not know any particular thing? Yes, God can choose not to know certain things.

There are two other instances where God clearly chooses *not* to know something. Jesus specifically said that only the Father knew when he would return to claim his bride.[1] God also said he will *not* remember our sins if we ask him to forgive us.

> [36] "But concerning that day and hour no one knows, not even the angels of heaven, nor the Son, but the Father only. [37] For as were the days of Noah, so will be the coming of the Son of Man. (Matt. 24:36–37 ESV)

> [34] And no longer shall each one teach his neighbor and each his brother, saying, 'Know the LORD,' for they shall all know me, from the least of them to the greatest, declares the LORD. For I will forgive their iniquity, and I will remember their sin no more." (Jer. 31:34 ESV)

> [16] "This is the covenant that I will make with them
>   after those days, declares the Lord:
> I will put my laws on their hearts,
>   and write them on their minds,"
> [17] then he adds,
> "I will remember their sins and their lawless deeds no more." (Heb. 10:16–17 ESV)

---

[1] Ron Smith, *Between Justice and Mercy*, "How We Became the Bride of Christ."

Beyond choosing not to know a thing, how does God create men with unique personalities? Surely he would have to tinker with our psyches. But he didn't. He gave our *selves* to us. What happens in our life is a product of bad choices, inherited sinful nature, and the broken world we live in. What we *can* become is what we let him make of us, despite our dire circumstances.

He didn't *force* us to be sinful, just like he didn't *force* us to love him. Yet with all the chaos we have made of ourselves and our world, God knew we were *worth* creating. Only he is powerful enough to create the way he did.

In 1 Corinthians 13:8 (KJV), God says love never fails. We *are* his children—not his robots—in whom he takes great pleasure. He will *never* stop loving us whatever choices we make.

CHAPTER THREE

God's Plan

Was God surprised when Adam and Eve disobeyed and separated themselves from him? Did he anticipate our failure? What about angels? Did they have a choice, too? Can God save the fallen angels?

Not a Rescue Plan. I have watched Lee Strobel's *The Case for Faith* countless times. Greg Koukl, of Stand to Reason, is one of his interviewees. I have often thought about this one comment Koukl makes.

> "Because this justice of God is perfect, this separation should have lasted for eternity," says Strobel.

> "But there's hope," says Koukl. "God didn't just leave it at that, though he might have. Out of love, <u>he reached down with a rescue effort</u>."

I've not discussed this with Mr. Koukl or Mr. Strobel, men I admire and respect. Without being critical, I think Koukl is unintentionally incorrect. The word "rescue" seems to imply surprise. Is it possible that God created man only to be suddenly surprised by his disobedience? I don't think so. Otherwise, God is not timeless.[1]

Eternity is time bound and began when everything was created. Outside of time, God sees all points as though they are the same moment. He knew

---

[1] Ron Smith, *Between Justice and Mercy*, "Timelessness."

"before" he created us, we would fail. His plan all along was to redeem us. He wasn't surprised at all.

God still called his creation "good" knowing full well what we would do. Declaring creation good was not a "pat-on-the-back" comment either. God has *no* pride to hurt, and no one had yet been created to observe his act of creation as far as we know. Though we don't know when he created angels, we know from Genesis 2:1 that all he created on earth, he created in those six days.

⌗

Men and Angels. God created man with a body, soul, and spirit, knowing nothing about the consequences of good and evil. Adam and Eve had children, and their children had children, and so on. Over time, all the people that ever were, are, or will be, came from the first two.

As far as we know, God created all the angels at one time in the beginning. Scripture does not indicate that angels beget other angels, and they are entirely spirit and soul. Lucifer was created on a day, but Scripture gives no particulars Logically, I suspect angels and men came into existence at the same moment. Angels from their creation knew good and evil precisely as God did, while men knew nothing. We infer that from the way the serpent spoke in the garden of Eden. That's the reason God can redeem us, but he cannot save fallen angels.

Both men and angels can and have rejected God. At present, we don't fully understand what sin and separation from God does to us. Read what Jesus said about God's swift and final justice on Lucifer. Revelation 12:4 suggests that he took a third of the angels when he was cast down. The consequences of his sin are not pretty.

[17] The seventy-two returned with joy, saying, "Lord, even the demons are subject to us in your name!"
[18] And he said to them, "I saw Satan fall like lightning from heaven.
[19] Behold, I have given you authority to tread on serpents and scorpions, and over all the power of the enemy, and nothing shall hurt you.
[20] Nevertheless, do not rejoice in this, that the spirits are subject to you,

but rejoice that your names are written in heaven." (Luke 10:17–20 ESV)

¹² "How you are fallen from heaven,
    O Day Star, son of Dawn!
How you are cut down to the ground,
    you who laid the nations low!
¹³ You said in your heart,
    'I will ascend to heaven;
above the stars of God
    I will set my throne on high;
I will sit on the mount of assembly
    in the far reaches of the north;
¹⁴ I will ascend above the heights of the clouds;
    I will make myself like the Most High.'
¹⁵ But you are brought down to Sheol,
    to the far reaches of the pit.
¹⁶ Those who see you will stare at you
    and ponder over you:
'Is this the man who made the earth tremble,
    who shook kingdoms,
¹⁷ who made the world like a desert
    and overthrew its cities,
    who did not let his prisoners go home?'
¹⁸ All the kings of the nations lie in glory,
    each in his own tomb;
¹⁹ but you are cast out, away from your grave,
    like a loathed branch,
clothed with the slain, those pierced by the sword,
    who go down to the stones of the pit,
    like a dead body trampled underfoot.
²⁰ You will not be joined with them in burial,
    because you have destroyed your land,
    you have slain your people.
"May the offspring of evildoers
    nevermore be named!
    (Isa. 14:12–20 ESV)

¹¹ Moreover, the word of the LORD came to me: ¹² "Son of man, raise a lamentation over the king of Tyre, and say to him, Thus says the Lord GOD:
    "You were the signet of perfection,
        full of wisdom and perfect in beauty.
¹³ You were in Eden, the garden of God;
        every precious stone was your covering,

sardius, topaz, and diamond,
 beryl, onyx, and jasper,
  sapphire, emerald, and carbuncle;
 and crafted in gold were your settings
 and your engravings.
On the day that you were created
 they were prepared.
[14] You were an anointed guardian cherub.
 I placed you; you were on the holy mountain of God;
 in the midst of the stones of fire you walked.
[15] You were blameless in your ways
 from the day you were created,
 till unrighteousness was found in you.
[16] In the abundance of your trade
 you were filled with violence in your midst, and you sinned;
 so I cast you as a profane thing from the mountain of God,
 and I destroyed you, O guardian cherub,
 from the midst of the stones of fire.
[17] Your heart was proud because of your beauty;
 you corrupted your wisdom for the sake of your splendor.
I cast you to the ground;
 I exposed you before kings,
 to feast their eyes on you.
[18] By the multitude of your iniquities,
 in the unrighteousness of your trade
 you profaned your sanctuaries;
 so I brought fire out from your midst;
  it consumed you,
 and I turned you to ashes on the earth
 in the sight of all who saw you.
[19] All who know you among the peoples
 are appalled at you;
you have come to a dreadful end
 and shall be no more forever."
(Ezek. 28:11 ESV)

Why is it that God offers mercy to mankind but not to angels? Why did God make us different? He loves us both. Whatever his reasons, God intentionally made only man in *his* image. Angels and demons look quite different from us in the Bible.

The first family started with Adam and Eve, who had children. Their sons begat children and started families, and so on over generations. Each person seems to be created at particular points along time, while for God they are created all at once. Over our life we come to know and understand good and evil, and that we are separated from God.

Two things seem to make men different. First, we were ignorant of good and evil when we sinned. Second, we were made in God's image with a physical body patterned after Jesus Christ's body. We develop and change spiritually, mentally, and physically throughout our life. Angels are also trapped in time, but they didn't learn good and evil the way Adam and Eve did. Their disobedience proceeded out of a complete understanding of good and evil.

Because men beget men after their own biologic form, God can physically insert himself into mankind in the person of Jesus Christ. Adam's sinful nature could not be passed down to Jesus. Though he is genealogically in Adam's line, he is not biologically his son. Jesus is unique in all creation because he is Mary's child and the Son of God.

Angels don't beget angels. They have no human form and are not made in the image of God the way we are. Because of their complete understanding of good and evil and fully developed personality from their creation, any *one* trespass means permanent separation from God. Thus, those angels, which are now demons, are irretrievably lost.

I admit this might at first sound harsh, but consider this. A rebellious child does not grasp that actions have consequences until those actions have resulted in consequences. A rebellious angel, on the other hand, knowing full well what the consequences of their actions would be, made a determined decision to rebel.

Writing himself into the stream of mankind's story began God's effort to redeem us. God's redemption plan for us hinged on two logical options. He could judge and condemn us, or we could pay the price to regain our holiness and return to fellowship with him. If he condemns us, then we are separated from him forever. The catch in the second option is that if we pay the price, the penalty of death still separates us from him forever. *Every* man would have to die for themselves, and all men would still suffer separation.

If the penalty requires separation resulting in death, then the only way to save us is for God to write himself into our story and become a man. That man is Jesus Christ who is the Son of God, yet fully man. Because he is both holy and human, he can represent all men. He alone can pay the penalty for all of us.

Only the Son of God can withstand his own justice *and* live again. He dies, but because he is holy, his Father will not let him see corruption; he raises him from death. Because he is our representative—our substitute—Jesus can represent us all. Once we accept him as our representative, our price is paid, and he will also raise us up human but holy. Despite a saving alternative, some men will choose to remain separated. He gives both men and angels a choice within the context of the nature of their being.

> [10] For you will not abandon my soul to *Sheol*,
>   or let your holy one see corruption.
> (Ps. 16:10 ESV)

> [27] For you will not abandon my soul to Hades,
>   or let your Holy One see corruption.
> (Acts 2:27 ESV)

> [13] Therefore he says also in another psalm,
>   "'You will not let your Holy One see corruption.'
> (Acts 13:35 ESV)

Why must all sin result in a death? Can't God just leave us alone to continue doing our own thing?

God can *never* sin; that kind of nature is called holiness. Like water and oil, sin never mixes with holiness. A sinful nature drives us to separate ourselves from him. The prodigal son didn't leave because his father told him to go.

Separation from God is not like two people being in different rooms of a house. Rather, it is when one of the persons is oblivious to the presence of the other in the same room as a ghost. God will leave us alone and, in that sense; we will be oblivious to him forever. He grieves so much because he can never be oblivious to us. Because he is everywhere, he will have to endure watching us suffer forever, consumed by the willful choice of our sinful nature.

Lewis's work of fiction, *The Magician's Nephew*, touches on this.

> "Oh—Aslan, sir," said Digory, turning red, "I forgot to tell you. The Witch has already eaten one of those apples, one of the same kind that Tree grew from." He hadn't really said all he was thinking, but Polly at once said it for him. (Digory was always much more afraid than she of looking a fool.)
>
> "So we thought, Aslan," she said, "that there must be some mistake, and she can't really mind the smell of those apples."
>
> "Why do you think that, Daughter of Eve?" asked the Lion.
>
> "Well, she ate one."
>
> "Child," he replied, "that is why all the rest are now a horror to her. That is what happens to those who pluck and eat fruits at the wrong time and in the wrong way. The fruit is good, but they loathe it ever after."
>
> "Oh I see," said Polly. "And I suppose because she took it in the wrong way it won't work for her. I mean, it won't make her always young and all that?"
>
> "Alas," said Aslan, shaking his head. "It will. Things always work according to their nature. She has won her heart's desire; she has unwearying strength and endless days like a goddess. But length of days with an evil heart is only length of misery, and already she begins to know it. <u>All get what they want; they do not always like it</u>."

Men and angels are not a mistake. God loves his creation. His plan to redeem us was not an afterthought.

CHAPTER FOUR

Heaven and Hell

What happens after we die? Are we going to heaven, hell, or some other in-between state? Will we just cease to exist?

Fear of Hell. We all spend a great deal of time every day thinking about what will happen to us. Uncertainty pursues us, and it torments many. Just look at those who have an unfounded fear of germs or leaving their homes. I think often our adult fears escalate from typical childhood anxieties. Regardless, fear enters into much of our thinking.

At ages six and seven, my granddaughters liked to sleep with my wife and me in the RV trailer. They insisted we leave as many lights on as we could. It didn't matter that in seconds they would be asleep and oblivious to the light.

In their minds, the light kept the bogey man away even while they slept. No matter how much we reassured them, they would not be convinced that the light was not protecting their slumber—we were.

As we become adults, things can get worse. We juggle and push our fears around in our heads like children who keep the lights on. Fear is a predator that prowls the recesses of our mind, stalking our peace. So we try to put fears out of our mind "by leaving the lights on."

As we get older, fewer and fewer days lie ahead as the number of bygone days grows. We naturally think about death much more often, and we cannot push that out so easily. It isn't really death we fear so much, but the unknown that follows.

I have heard it said that animals flee because they are being pursued. Being caught is what drives them to run, not really the thought of death. Man is different. Death pursues us, but we know keenly that something lies beyond. It is the unknown hereafter that prowls our minds.

The fear of hell is that way. It isn't so much death itself we fear. It is the sting of death, the unknown consequence after we pass.

Separation is the Decision. This section of Scripture has always intrigued me, especially because Jesus was the one telling the story. It does not sound like a parable, but something Jesus had personally observed and was relating.

> [19] "There was a rich man who was clothed in purple and fine linen and who feasted sumptuously every day. [20] And at his gate was laid a poor man named Lazarus, covered with sores, [21] who desired to be fed with what fell from the rich man's table. Moreover, even the dogs came and licked his sores.
> [22] The poor man died and was carried by the angels to Abraham's side. The rich man also died and was buried, [23] and in Hades, being in torment, he lifted up his eyes and saw Abraham far off and Lazarus at his side. [24] And he called out, 'Father Abraham, have mercy on me, and send Lazarus to dip the end of his finger in water and cool my tongue, for I am in anguish in this flame.'
> [25] But Abraham said, 'Child, remember that you in your lifetime received your good things, and Lazarus in like manner bad things; but now he is comforted here, and you are in anguish. [26] And besides all this, between us and you a great chasm has been fixed, in order that those who would pass from here to you may not be able, and none may cross from there to us.'
> [27] And he said, 'Then I beg you, father, to send him to my father's house — [28] for I have five brothers—so that he may warn them, lest they also come into this place of torment.'
> [29] But Abraham said, 'They have Moses and the Prophets; let them hear them.' [30] And he said, 'No, father Abraham, but if someone goes to them from the dead, they will repent.' [31] He said to him, 'If they do not hear Moses and the Prophets, neither will they be convinced if someone should rise from the dead.'" (Luke 16:19–31 ESV)

We know that riches can be a great stumbling block in a relationship with God. Why depend on God if you have wealth. Though the wealth and poverty are notable details in this story, being rich or poor is not the point.

Cleary the rich man knows why he is there, because he asks Abraham to warn his brothers. Notice that the rich man *never* asks Abraham to take him out of hell? The only reason for that must be that he fully understood and embraced his choice. All he wanted was something to cool his tongue. His rejection of God was so final, even the pain of hell could not make him ask for mercy.

Where is God when the rich man cries out for relief? Just like Aslan was there with the dwarves, imprisoned in that awful stable in *The Last Battle*—God is there! Like the dwarves, the rich man has blinded himself. Their rejection is insurmountable.

> ⁷ <u>Where shall I go from your Spirit?</u>
> <u>Or where shall I flee from your presence?</u>
> ⁸ If I ascend to heaven, you are there!
> If I make my bed in *Sheol*, you are there!
> ⁹ If I take the wings of the morning
> and dwell in the uttermost parts of the sea,
> ¹⁰ even there your hand shall lead me,
> and your right hand shall hold me.
> ¹¹ If I say, "Surely the darkness shall cover me,
> and the light about me be night,"
> ¹² even the darkness is not dark to you;
> the night is bright as the day,
> for darkness is as light with you.
> (Ps. 139:7-12 ESV)

Could God force them into a relationship with him? The synonym for forced love is *slavery*. Because the dwarves refused to be changed, he gave them over to their desires. He loved them so much that he would not force anything on them. All get what they want, even the rich man.

> ²⁸ And since they did not see fit to acknowledge God, God gave them up to a debased mind to do what ought not to be done. ²⁹ They were filled with all manner of unrighteousness, evil, covetousness, malice. They are full of envy, murder, strife, deceit, maliciousness. They are gossips, ³⁰ slanderers, haters of God, insolent, haughty, boastful, inventors of evil,

disobedient to parents, [31] foolish, faithless, heartless, ruthless. [32] Though they know God's righteous decree that those who practice such things deserve to die, they not only do them but give approval to those who practice them. (Rom. 1:28–32 ESV)

Even in giving way to the rich man's desires, God's heart does not let go. He still wants and loves him. Put aside the controversy about whether Jesus is preaching to everyone dead and ponder this verse. Why else would Jesus be preaching in hell if he was not grieved by it all.

> [18] For Christ also suffered once for sins, the righteous for the unrighteous, that he might bring us to God, being put to death in the flesh but made alive in the spirit, [19] in which he went and proclaimed [or *preached*] to the spirits in prison, [20] because they formerly did not obey, when God's patience waited in the days of Noah, while the ark was being prepared, in which a few, that is, eight persons, were brought safely through water. (1 Peter 3:18–20 ESV)

Abraham and the rich man, though separated by a great gulf, did communicate. Does anyone in hell listen, repent, and try to cross over that chasm? Sadly, I think not. If Jesus did preach to hell, no one on the wrong side of the chasm was listening.

I'm again reminded of the dwarves in the shed who only heard a lion roar when Aslan tried to talk to them. What did hell's occupants here when Jesus spoke? Like the dwarves with Aslan, they could not see Jesus, much less hear him. Their own mind shackled them there.

The story of the rich man and Lazarus suggests that the minds of those who separate themselves in hell across that great chasm can never again be breached. Their rejection and spiritual deafness are final. They get what they want. God's love requires that he abandon them to their awful choice.

Why would the Son of God continue to want to forgive when there is no possibility of success?

This Scripture in Peter strongly supports the Circle of Love; his love is truly never-ending. God hates the sin that we all commit, but he loves us forever.

He has the power to change hearts and minds and forgive those who reject him, *if* they would but grant him the license to do so.

The walls of human rejection are impenetrable. As persistent and powerful as he is, the hound of heaven[1] cannot bound past that barrier. That's also why a loving, good, and all-powerful God cannot simply snap his finger and eliminate evil, suffering, and unhappiness in our world.

He loves us so much, that he *must* allow us to have our way and die without him. The sting of death produces torment, because we were not made to be without God.

⚜

Fellowship with God. Why do we want to go to heaven? For many, the answer is that they simply don't want to go to hell. They choose heaven out of fear of hell and the hope of a better place than earth with no pain. No doubt it must, after all, be the better option.

Like my granddaughters, it is as though "the light is on," but in their slumber, the impending darkness is really just out of sight and out of mind. Many think they have faith and believe that they are saved, but what they really mean is they *hope* they will not go to hell. They just don't know for sure, because they are trusting they measure up and will get in.

If anyone really thinks choosing heaven over hell boils down to an afterlife of bliss or torment, they have missed the point altogether. Life is not just marching day by day to the end, when death brings us to the final fork of the road with the sign for heaven on the right and hell on the left. It isn't about *where* we will be or even about bliss or torment; it is about *who* we choose to be with.

God loves us, but he does not need us. He *wants* to be with us. Nothing is required to receive his love other than to reach out a hand of acceptance. To

---

[1] Francis Thompson, "The Hound of Heaven," in *The Oxford Book of English Mystical Verse.*

fully understand how God's love works, we need look no further than ancient Jewish wedding ritual and the love of a bridegroom for his bride.

There are three parts to the ancient Jewish matrimonial process which took from three to seven years.[2] Modern Jewish and Christian marriage traditions reverse these parts. Initially, the father, or other representative of the bridegroom, would approach the father of the bride with a proposal of marriage. Weddings were not arranged per se, as the bride's father would ask her if she was amenable. If she was, then the two families would strike a contractural agreement in a written document called a *ketubah*.

That initiated the first part of the wedding ceremony called the *shiddukhin*. The *ketubah* was not a modern prenuptial agreement. Giving up a daughter meant significant economic loss to the family. Its purpose was to set the bride-price called the *mohar*. It also specified how much the husband gave his bride if he later divorced her. The bride was responsible only for her purity, and the bridegroom was not entitled to a dowry.

Ketubah were religious documents and legally binding. The legally sealed copy was stored in the local synagogues. Marriage was about family, children, faithfulness and above all, love. The *ketubah* also preserved family genealogy. These scrolls are how we know Jesus's lineage through both Joseph[3] and Mary.[4] Because they were not preserved like the Dead Sea Scrolls, few, if any, ancient originals exist today.

Once the *ketubah* was signed, the couple were spiritually, socially, and legally married, and separation required a legal divorce. However, the husband and wife did not yet consummate physically. The bride's purity was extremely significant now. Mary became pregnant[5] after her *ketubah* signing, and she could have been stoned.[6] Joseph must have loved her dearly, because by law he would've cast the first stone.

---

[2] Ron Smith, *Between Justice and Mercy*, "How We Became the Bride of Christ."
[3] Matt. 1:2–16.
[4] Luke 3:23–38.
[5] Ron Smith, *Between Justice and Mercy*, "How We Became the Bride of Christ."
[6] Deut. 22:20–21 ESV.

The *shiddukhin* lasted from one to two years. The bridegroom busily worked on building new living quarters for them off of his father's house. The bride continued to live in her father's house. At a time deemed appropriate by the bridegroom's father, he would send his son to the bride's father's house. This second part constituted the *erusin*.

The bridegroom first paid the bride-price to her father Then she and he entered a room called the *chuppah* chamber where they physically consummated. Outside the door of the room, their witnesses stood ready. She would lie on a white cloth called a *chuppah*. During intercourse, her virginal hymen would be torn and bleed onto the cloth. As soon as the bridegroom saw the blood, he would begin to rejoice and yell loudly. Upon hearing his joyful cries, the witnesses outside the door would join his caterwauling celebration.

After the *erusin*, the bridegroom returned to his father's house and continued to work on their living quarters. The bride remained in her father's house, and no further physical intimacy followed until the wedding feast called the *nissuin*.

Several more years could elapse before the *nissuin*, which began when the bridegroom's father, without notice, sent his son to bring his bride home. Suddenly and without warning, the bridegroom appears at her front door and lawfully takes her back to his father's house, where the great celebratory *nissuin* feast is ready with many guests present. The whole ancient marriage practice could take up to seven years. Jacob waited seven years each for Leah and Rachel.

Jesus is the bridegroom, and ancient Jewish wedding tradition is a *figura umbra* of him and the church. Our *ketubah* has been signed. The Last Supper represents the bride-price and the chuppah blood of the *erusin*. The church is now waiting patiently for the Father to instruct his Son to retrieve her for the *nissuin* wedding feast.

Not all will get into that feast, though. Theirs will be the story of hell and not heaven. Those who have not accepted Christ's forgiveness with be like the five foolish virgins.

> [1] "Then the kingdom of heaven will be like ten virgins who took their lamps and went to meet the bridegroom. [2] Five of them were foolish, and five were wise. [3] For when the foolish took their lamps, they took no oil with them, [4] but the wise took flasks of oil with their lamps. [5] As the bridegroom was delayed, they all became drowsy and slept.
> [6] But at midnight there was a cry, 'Here is the bridegroom! Come out to meet him.'
> [7] Then all those virgins rose and trimmed their lamps. [8] And the foolish said to the wise, 'Give us some of your oil, for our lamps are going out.'
> [9] But the wise answered, saying, 'Since there will not be enough for us and for you, go rather to the dealers and buy for yourselves.'
> [10] And while they were going to buy, the bridegroom came, and those who were ready went in with him to the marriage feast, and the door was shut.
> [11] Afterward the other virgins came also, saying, 'Lord, lord, open to us.'
> [12] But he answered, 'Truly, I say to you, I do not know you.'
> [13] Watch therefore, for you know neither the day nor the hour. (Matt. 25:1-13 ESV)

Where is hell? It is a place without God's perceived presence. There, people will be undisturbed by his voice or his presence, yet tormented by their own nature. Where is heaven? It is the place where God is. He is the real prize—not heaven!

All get what they want. They do not always like it.

CHAPTER FIVE

Is God in Control

In the mid-1990s, the song *God Is in Control*[1] dominated Christian music and thinking. I liked the song, but I don't like how its popularity hinged on the catch-phrase title. Often, well-meaning believers shielded their personal fears without understanding what God's control is and is not. Is God really in control of the smallest aspect of our lives?

The Judge Does Right. The following Scripture seems to be evidence that God limits his control at some point. If God wanted absolute control of Abraham, why did God reason with him? Certainly the events of his life did not take a timeless God by surprise.

In this back-and-forth exchange with God, I've often wondered if Abraham could have continued to negotiate the number of righteous men down to five or even less. Were Abraham's thoughts even under God's control? Was ten just God's magic boundary?

> [22] So the men turned from there and went toward Sodom, but Abraham still stood before the LORD. [23] Then Abraham drew near and said, "Will you indeed sweep away the righteous with the wicked? [24] Suppose there are fifty righteous within the city. Will you then sweep away the place and not spare it for the fifty righteous who are in it? [25] Far be it from you to do such a thing, to put the righteous to death with the wicked, so that the righteous fare as the wicked! Far be that from you! Shall not the Judge of all the earth do what is just?"

---

[1] Twila Paris, *God is in Control.* On *Beyond A Dream*, 1994. Album.

[26] And the LORD said, "If I find at Sodom fifty righteous in the city, I will spare the whole place for their sake." (Gen. 18:22–26 ESV)

God dealt no differently with Hezekiah. Why reason with someone over whom you have absolute control?

[1] In those days Hezekiah became sick and was at the point of death. And Isaiah the prophet the son of Amoz came to him and said to him, "Thus says the LORD, 'Set your house in order, for you shall die; you shall not recover.'"
[2] Then Hezekiah turned his face to the wall and prayed to the LORD, saying, [3] "Now, O LORD, please remember how I have walked before you in faithfulness and with a whole heart, and have done what is good in your sight." And Hezekiah wept bitterly.
[4] And before Isaiah had gone out of the middle court, the word of the LORD came to him: [5] "Turn back, and say to Hezekiah the leader of my people, Thus says the LORD, the God of David your father: I have heard your prayer; I have seen your tears. Behold, I will heal you. On the third day you shall go up to the house of the LORD, [6] and I will add fifteen years to your life. I will deliver you and this city out of the hand of the king of Assyria, and I will defend this city for my own sake and for my servant David's sake."
[7] And Isaiah said, "Bring a cake of figs. And let them take and lay it on the boil, that he may recover." (2 Kings 20:1–7 ESV)

On a personal level, God does not control these two men like tethered robots. He cannot have any relationship, much less a loving one, with a mindless robot. If he controlled us like robots, then any exchange of so-called love would be meaningless.

On the other hand, he can require us to obey or repent and change our evil ways without controlling us. He can prevent us from sinning to a point, but ultimately we can override that protection. His core of agape love *must* allow us the freedom to disobey.

[18] "Come now, let us reason together, says the LORD:
  though your sins are like scarlet,
    they shall be as white as snow;
  though they are red like crimson,
    they shall become like wool.
[19] If you are willing and obedient,
    you shall eat the good of the land;
[20] but if you refuse and rebel,

> you shall be eaten by the sword;
> for the mouth of the LORD has spoken."
> (Isa. 1:18–20 ESV)

Can God indeed be in control and at the same time *not* be in control? Those are mutually exclusive at the lowest individual level. Why does God control some things and not others?

The scope to his control depends on the object. He deals with kingdoms and the offices of kings and lords with different control than individual people. He is perfectly capable of swaying the heart of a king while limiting individual control of thoughts and actions.

His influence on the course of mankind as a whole cannot be understated. Take, for example, when he confused the languages at the Tower of Babel. That accomplished a level of protective control, averting serious consequences without impinging on the individuals in such a way that they were deprived of choice. In Mark, he asserts control by cutting short the days of tribulation and all for the good of man.

> [1] Now the whole earth had one language and the same words. [2] And as people migrated from the east, they found a plain in the land of Shinar and settled there. [3] And they said to one another, "Come, let us make bricks, and burn them thoroughly." And they had brick for stone, and bitumen for mortar. [4] Then they said, "Come, let us build ourselves a city and a tower with its top in the heavens, and let us make a name for ourselves, lest we be dispersed over the face of the whole earth." [5] And the LORD came down to see the city and the tower, which the children of man had built. [6] And the LORD said, "Behold, they are one people, and they have all one language, and this is only the beginning of what they will do. And nothing that they propose to do will now be impossible for them. [7] Come, let us go down and there confuse their language, so that they may not understand one another's speech." [8] So the LORD dispersed them from there over the face of all the earth, and they left off building the city. [9] Therefore its name was called Babel, because there the LORD confused the language of all the earth. And from there the LORD dispersed them over the face of all the earth. (Gen. 11:1–9 ESV)

> [16] and let the one who is in the field not turn back to take his cloak. [17] And alas for women who are pregnant and for those who are nursing infants in those days! [18] Pray that it may not happen in winter. [19] For in

those days there will be such tribulation as has not been from the beginning of the creation that God created until now, and never will be. [20] And if the Lord had not cut short the days, no human being would be saved. But for the sake of the elect, whom he chose, he shortened the days. [21] And then if anyone says to you, 'Look, here is the Christ!' or 'Look, there he is!' do not believe it. [22] For false christs and false prophets will arise and perform signs and wonders, to lead astray, if possible, the elect. [23] But be on guard; I have told you all things beforehand. (Mark 13:16–23 ESV)

Exodus 4:21 is a verse which is often quoted to support the belief that God exercises control over the very hearts of men. Notice that further in Exodus it also says that Pharaoh hardened his own heart.

[21] And the LORD said to Moses, "When you go back to Egypt, see that you do before Pharaoh all the miracles that I have put in your power. But I will harden his heart, so that he will not let the people go. (Ex. 4:21 ESV)

[15] But when Pharaoh saw that there was a respite, he hardened his heart and would not listen to them, as the LORD had said. (Ex. 8:15 ESV)

Which is it? Does God do the hardening or does Pharaoh harden his own heart? Was Pharaoh good until God made him evil?

Exodus 4:21 is also often cherry-picked by those who believe fully in the idea that God chooses each of us to be a winner or loser, i.e., saved or lost. That is the ultimate level of control. This is innocently misguided at best and intentionally deceptive at worst. Such Scripture cherry-picking is dangerous because one can make the Bible say things that it does not say in order to make it fit a personal agenda. Look at these Scriptures.

[1] The king's heart is a stream of water in the hand of the LORD;
    he turns it wherever he will.
[2] Every way of a man is right in his own eyes,
    but the LORD weighs the heart.
(Prov. 21:1–2 ESV)

[1] From there Abraham journeyed toward the territory of the Negeb and lived between Kadesh and Shur; and he sojourned in Gerar. [2] And Abraham said of Sarah his wife, "She is my sister." And Abimelech king

of Gerar sent and took Sarah.

³ But God came to Abimelech in a dream by night and said to him, "Behold, you are a dead man because of the woman whom you have taken, for she is a man's wife."

⁴ Now Abimelech had not approached her. So he said, "Lord, will you kill an innocent people? ⁵ Did he not himself say to me, 'She is my sister'? And she herself said, 'He is my brother.' In the integrity of my heart and the innocence of my hands I have done this."

⁶ Then God said to him in the dream, "Yes, I know that you have done this in the integrity of your heart, and it was I who kept you from sinning against me. Therefore I did not let you touch her. ⁷ Now then, return the man's wife, for he is a prophet, so that he will pray for you, and you shall live. But if you do not return her, know that you shall surely die, you and all who are yours." (Gen. 20:1–7 ESV)

These verses paint a much different picture of how God can influence men. In the context of Proverbs here, God turns a man's heart as a stream. Most streams change course over the years as sediments accumulate and reroute its path of flow. What if that river that has been dammed up so as to completely control its flow and flooding?

Context makes all the difference. In Genesis, it seems God prevents Abimelech from sinning. Notice, though in the last verse, that Abimelech still has the choice to disobey.

Does God control just some people and not others? Did he pick Pharaoh to be a loser and Abimelech to be a winner? Does God ever say that he has varying respect for *any* person? Consider these two Scriptures as you ponder this.

¹⁵ Ye shall do no unrighteousness in judgment: thou shalt not respect the person of the poor, nor honour the person of the mighty: but in righteousness shalt thou judge thy neighbour. (Lev. 19:15 KJV)

²⁴ Knowing that of the Lord ye shall receive the reward of the inheritance: for ye serve the Lord Christ. ²⁵ But he that doeth wrong shall receive for the wrong which he hath done: and there is no respect of persons. (Col. 3:24–25 KJV)

When we say God is in control, we mean one of two things. Either God controls us down to the very thoughts we think and thus the salvation that he may sovereignly grant or deny us, or he controls the circumstances around us without controlling any individuals.

If the first option were so, then why would evil even be present? God would simply have eliminated it. The second option is the only one from which we can trace our current evil world.

More importantly, God *cannot* control us individually because it violates his core character of love. As I've already shown, God's character is not subject to the dimension of his sovereignty. He distributes mercy and justice equally and rightly. God does nothing arbitrarily, as he must do if he controls the smallest individual actions.

God can try to *influence* us to make the right choice, but the scope of that influence has a boundary beyond which his character *cannot* cross. While he knows our every thought, his influence amounts to gentle nudges. We make our ultimate decisions. Lewis implies this in *The Silver Chair*.[2]

> "Why were you so near the edge, Human Child?"
> "I was showing off, Sir."
> "That is a very good answer, Human Child. Do so no more. And now" (here for the first time the Lion's face became a little less stern) "the Boy is safe. I have blown him to Narnia. But your task will be the harder because of what you have done."
> "Please, what task, Sir?" said Jill.
> "The task for which I called you and him here out of your own world."
> This puzzled Jill very much. "It's mistaking me for someone else," she thought. She didn't dare to tell the Lion this, though she felt things would get into a dreadful muddle unless she did.
> "Speak your thought, Human Child," said the Lion.
> "I was wondering—I mean—could there be some mistake? Because nobody called me and Scrubb, you know. It was we who asked to come here. Scrubb said we were to call to—to Somebody—it was a name I wouldn't know—and perhaps the Somebody would let us in. And we did, and then we found the door open."
> "You would not have called to me unless I had been calling to you," said the Lion.
> "Then you are Somebody, Sir?" said Jill.

---

[2] C. S. Lewis, *The Silver Chair*.

"I am." [said Aslan.]

God sends blessing even upon the just and unjust.[3] Were his control minute, he would not do that. He would arbitrarily curse those whom he had chosen to curse and bless those whom he had chosen to bless.

C. S. Lewis made this statement in *The Problem of Pain*.[4]

> The sacrifice of Christ is repeated, or re-echoed, among His followers in very varying degrees, from the cruelest martyrdom down to a self-submission of intention whose outward signs have nothing to distinguish them from the ordinary fruits of temperance and reasonableness. The causes of this distribution I do not know; but from our present point of view it ought to be clear that the real problem is not why some humble, pious, believing people suffer, but why some do not.

If God is not controlling either Pharaoh or Abimelech, then why was one man's heart hardened and the other softened if he respects them equally? Isn't Pharaoh's and Abimelech's story really what Lewis is saying about pain here? Some suffer intensely and others don't and the reason is unknown to us. God gets blame for not controlling us and also for controlling us at the same time.

Pharaoh's heart was hardened because God could not gently influence him. Sometimes we harden our own hearts and become stiff-necked simply because we sense his Spirit speaking to us. God's mere presence is abhorrent to some, and as a result they choose to harden their heart.

The whole exercise with Pharaoh was not to inflict justice, but rather to offer mercy. What if Egypt had repented like Nineveh?[5] The painful plagues were God's last attempt to sway Egypt's heart. He is willing to use whatever it takes in our broken world, because he knows how much is at stake.

But like Pharaoh, we have the final say. We will all have to confess that God nudged us to himself the easiest way that we would come. That does not mean

---

[3] Matt. 5:44 ESV.
[4] C. S. Lewis, *The Problem of Pain*.
[5] Jonah 3:1–5.

all our troubles are over if we come to him. This present evil we endure is the consequence of past choices.

In the end, we can have a relationship with God where he promises to restore us. That matters most.

CHAPTER SIX

Three and Me

Our culture revolves around love. We pursue it relentlessly. Love story plots dominate our movies, which churn new twists for the same old plot. A man sees a woman, and she sees him. They feel like they love each other. Their feelings are a mixture of emotions and possibilities. Doubtless they do feel *eros*. Are those romantic feelings dominated by what love they want to bestow or what they hope to receive?

Perichoresis. The late Nabeel Qureshi described how he came to understand the Trinity.[1] He was raised Muslim from his birth in Pakistan and came to live in the United States years before the infamous 9/11 attack in New York. Like me, he studied chemistry on his way to becoming a medical doctor.

He struggled with the concept of the Trinity greatly because Islam disavows it altogether. The Trinity includes the Fatherhood and Sonship of God, and by inference, the Holy Spirit. In Islam, God is One and only one.

In chemistry, we come to understand that the basic elements can bond one to another through the outer electrons that spin around an inner core of protons and neutrons. Electrons don't just spin around willy nilly, though. They occupy different levels within the whole spinning electron cloud.

[1] Nabeel Qureshi, *Seeking Allah, Finding Jesus.*

41

Each level requires more energy to spin the electron, so they always occupy positions at the lowest possible level. We describe this level of energy as a quantum of energy. Within each level, only a certain number of electrons are allowed.

Stable elements have specific numbers of electrons. Most elements don't have enough electrons to fill each level precisely. When that is so, one element can chemically bond with another by sharing electrons. When they share, both act as though they have filled the precise quota of electrons that each element requires.

Thus we can draw connecting lines between elements which represent these electron bonds. Here is the connection between the oxygen and hydrogen elements of the water molecule.

The lines between the oxygen and two hydrogen atoms represent electrons which are being shared. These electrons act like small particles spinning very, very fast, sometimes around the hydrogen nucleus, and sometimes around the oxygen nucleus.

Because they are spinning so fast, they also behave like a cloud. Electrons have features then of both a fast-moving particle and this mist-like cloud of negative charge.

Sometimes these clouds can form in circles. Benzene is a molecule with six carbon atoms forming a six-sided ring or hexagon. It looks like this when we draw it on paper.

Each corner of this six-sided hexagon ring is a carbon atom. The lines between them represent shared electrons. Notice that between three pairs of carbon atoms, there are two lines, instead of just one. This represents two shared electrons. We call these connections double bonds.

Remember that electrons act like particles and also like clouds. This molecule in particular forms a ring-like electron cloud. The electrons don't just share between two carbon atoms, but share in a cloud spread between all six carbons. We can show this cloud of electrons like this.

In actuality, both representations of benzene are correct. In the first image, the electrons are behaving like individual particles, while in the second image, they are behaving like a cloud of electrons.

This offers the best description of the Trinity. We know scripturally that there are three persons of God. And we know that there is one God. This is how we can represent God then.

The Father, Son, and Holy Spirit each occupy a corner of the triangle. But their loving relationship exists like a cloud between the three of them. In theological terms we call this perichoresis,[2] which is derived from a Greek word meaning to go around in rotation.

This perichoretic circle flows just as the original Greek implies. Each person of God gives and in turn receives love from the other. It is much like watching cake batter in an electric mixing bowl. As the batter near the center swirls, it also "falls" into the center and toward the bottom of the bowl. The mixer then sweeps the batter back up along the inner bowl surface. After it reaches the top, it is swept into the center of the bowl where it again falls toward the bottom.

The Father, Son, and Holy Spirit are inseparable. That's why God, in three persons, is also one God. When you say "God" you have also said, "Father, Son, and Holy Spirit." They are the same, and both phrases are correct. Below is a Gothic triskele window graphic which elegantly portrays perichoreo between the three persons of the Trinity.[3]

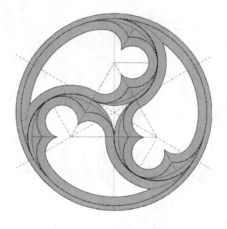

Justice or Mercy. In the Circle of Love graphic, justice, mercy, and love form a tight triangle. At its center, we are the object of all three. There in the center— there is safety and refuge. It is as if as we stand at the center of these three,

---

[2] Theopedia, "Perichoresis" https://www.theopedia.com/Perichoresis.
[3] Triskel Type Tonkedega, permission given by 1stEc.Domnowall, 2ndUser: Perhelion - tonquedec et église,melrand et chapelle,berrien et chapelle,cruas, CC BY-SA 3.0, https://commons.wikimedia.org/w/index.php?curid=18250014.

their arms locked, gazing as if they have eyes for no one else. We are protected as long as we do not leave the center of the triangle.

Within the triangle, the only thing that can take our gaze from the Trinity is unforgiveness. Being in the center however does not erase our memory of the trespasses against us. While God is able to forget individual sin, we cannot.

If we leave his triangular gaze, and unforgiveness creeps back into our heart, we can again become bitter and judgmental of the wrongs done to us. We become again what we once were, and it wrecks our soul, like a dog returning to its vomit.

> [23] "Therefore the kingdom of heaven may be compared to a king who wished to settle accounts with his servants. [24] When he began to settle, one was brought to him who owed him ten thousand talents. [25] And since he could not pay, his master ordered him to be sold, with his wife and children and all that he had, and payment to be made.
> [26] So the servant fell on his knees, imploring him, 'Have patience with me, and I will pay you everything.' [27] And out of pity for him, the master of that servant released him and forgave him the debt.
> [28] But when that same servant went out, he found one of his fellow servants who owed him a hundred denarii, and seizing him, he began to choke him, saying, 'Pay what you owe.'
> [29] So his fellow servant fell down and pleaded with him, 'Have patience with me, and I will pay you.'
> [30] He refused and went and put him in prison until he should pay the debt. [31] When his fellow servants saw what had taken place, they were greatly distressed, and they went and reported to their master all that had taken place.
> [32] Then his master summoned him and said to him, 'You wicked servant! I forgave you all that debt because you pleaded with me. [33] And should not you have had mercy on your fellow servant, as I had mercy on you?'
> [34] And in anger his master delivered him to the jailers, until he should pay all his debt.
> [35] So also my heavenly Father will do to every one of you, if you do not forgive your brother from your heart." (Matt. 18:23–35 ESV)

Such a departure from his gaze does not mean we have walked away. It does not necessarily mean we have become unbelievers again either. Staying within his focus is the struggle with which we all pursue. He knows this. Remember that the prodigal son was *not* apostate. We all have to walk back and ask forgiveness, and that is completely in our control.

⁷ But if we walk in the light, as he is in the light, we have fellowship with one another, and the blood of Jesus his Son cleanses us from all sin. ⁸ If we say we have no sin, we deceive ourselves, and the truth is not in us. ⁹ If we confess our sins, he is faithful and just to forgive us our sins and to cleanse us from all unrighteousness. (1 John 1:7–9 ESV)

Leaving God Forever. When we become the bride of Christ, nothing can remove us from him unless *we* choose to leave him forever. His promise is firm.

⁴ "What man of you, having a hundred sheep, if he has lost one of them, does not leave the ninety-nine in the open country, and go after the one that is lost, until he finds it? (Luke 15:4 ESV)

⁸ "Or what woman, having ten silver coins, if she loses one coin, does not light a lamp and sweep the house and seek diligently until she finds it? (Luke 15:8 ESV)

¹² While I was with them, I kept them in your name, which you have given me. I have guarded them, and not one of them has been lost except the son of destruction, that the Scripture might be fulfilled. (John 17:12 ESV)

⁹ This was to fulfill the word that he had spoken: "Of those whom you gave me I have lost not one." (John 18:9 ESV)

Why then does it say this in Hebrews?

¹ Therefore let us leave the elementary doctrine of Christ and go on to maturity, not laying again a foundation of repentance from dead works and of faith toward God, ² and of instruction about washings, the laying on of hands, the resurrection of the dead, and eternal judgment. ³ And this we will do if God permits. ⁴ For it is impossible, in the case of those who have once been enlightened, who have tasted the heavenly gift, and have shared in the Holy Spirit, ⁵ and have tasted the goodness of the word of God and the powers of the age to come, ⁶ and then have fallen away, to restore them again to repentance, since they are crucifying once again the Son of God to their own harm and holding him up to contempt. ⁷ For land that has drunk the rain that often falls on it, and produces a crop useful to those for whose sake it is cultivated, receives a blessing from God. ⁸ But if it bears thorns and thistles, it is worthless and near to being cursed, and its end is to be burned. (Heb. 6:1–8 ESV)

While we are presently in earthly bodies of flesh and blood, we can and will stray outside the center of God's gaze. He will forgive us again and again, always striving to put us back in the center of his perichoresis.

⁹ If we confess our sins, he is faithful and just to forgive us our sins and to cleanse us from all unrighteousness. (1 John 1:9 ESV)

The present for us is a process. But we will not always have to strive like we do now. There is coming a day when sin will no longer be able to even enter our mind. He has promised to complete the change that has begun us.

⁶ And I am sure of this, that he who began a good work in you will bring it to completion at the day of Jesus Christ. (Phil. 1:6 ESV)

⁵¹ Behold! I tell you a mystery. We shall not all sleep, but we shall all be changed, ⁵² in a moment, in the twinkling of an eye, at the last trumpet. For the trumpet will sound, and the dead will be raised imperishable, and we shall be changed. ⁵³ For this perishable body must put on the imperishable, and this mortal body must put on immortality. ⁵⁴ When the perishable puts on the imperishable, and the mortal puts on immortality, then shall come to pass the saying that is written:
"Death is swallowed up in victory."
⁵⁵ "O death, where is your victory?
O death, where is your sting?"
⁵⁶ The sting of death is sin, and the power of sin is the law. ⁵⁷ But thanks be to God, who gives us the victory through our Lord Jesus Christ. (1 Cor. 15:51–57 ESV)

How will we ever *not* be able to think an evil thought? This change is to us a mystery. God is nothing if not faithful to his Word.

Agape love does not hold us prisoner, however. It cannot be agape love if it did. Why do some choose to leave his triangular gaze? What is so different about knowing God, and then leaving him, compared to refusing him without ever having accepted his love?

It is critical to understand that God's relationship to us is truly like a marriage. Before marriage, we are not bound by any contract or covenant. As soon as we sign our own *ketubah* and become another member of his *bride*, only a divorce can separate us.

We can walk away from him, and he will let us. He cannot force us to love him.

Why anyone would first become a believer and then later walk away can only be answered within the heart of those that do, I think. We do know people who have professed apostasy and publicly walked away.

Apostasy is no mere story of a prodigal son. Leaving God takes a determination which must certainly be present until the very end of life. There is a point at which God knows there is nothing he can do to retrieve us. He finally gives us over to our own reprobation permanently.

Billy Graham and Charles Templeton were best friends and brothers in Christ when *Youth for Christ* first started. Lee Strobel tells the story in his movie *The Case for Faith*. Charles was slated to become one of the most significant evangelists in North America, and maybe the world. Alas, most people today don't even know his name.

After believing in Christ and walking and preaching in faith, determined doubt crept in. Templeton eventually rejected Christ. At 80, he published his book *Farewell to God: My Reasons for Rejecting the Christian Faith*. Accepting Christ is a marriage. If indeed Templeton once had accepted Christ, then his rejection is truly a divorce.

The ministry of Christ reflects the ancient Jewish wedding. Beginning with his *mikvah* baptism in the Jordan to the bride-price of the bread and the *chuppah* wine at the Last Supper, and on to the future wedding feast in heaven, we are married to our Lord. Bear in mind also, that Old Testament Scripture forbids a man having divorced his wife to take her again.

> [1] "If a man divorces his wife
>   and she goes from him
> and becomes another man's wife,
>   will he return to her?
> Would not that land be greatly polluted?
> You have played the whore with many lovers;
>   and would you return to me?

declares the LORD.
(Jer. 3:1 ESV)

Following his Passover death around 3 p.m. on 14 Nisan, they hastily buried Jesus. Three days passed. At dusk, 18 Nisan and the end of the weekly Sabbath, Jesus was raised from the dead, but his body was not the same as when he died. It was incorruptible and death can never again touch Jesus.

The point here is that Jesus *cannot* die again. His body has been forever changed. He cannot provide the blood for the *chuppah* cloth. There is no other sacrifice available for those having accepted his salvation, but later reject him.

Far be it from me or any man to judge Charles Templeton, even by his printed words. Only God and Templeton know his fate and whether he is truly gone for good. If he returned to Christ before his death, then certainly he was only prodigal and not apostate. Our Father is extremely patient and wise with his children.

God loves us so much that he will allow us to choose not to love him in return. It is only for him to say when that happens—but it *does* happen. All get what they want.

Personalities. Why are there three persons in one God? That question is often asked, but there is no answer. As we say about many things in life, *it is what it is!*

It is like asking why the sky is blue. Chemical analysis of the composition of the atmosphere leads us to observe that the interaction of light with a particular mixture of atoms *results* in a blue sky. But we still don't fundamentally understand *why*. Ultimately, God decided not only *what* would be blue, but what *blue* even means.

I remember early in childhood wondering if everyone else experienced the physical world exactly the way I did. When I felt pain, was everyone else's pain sensation just like mine? When I was sad or happy, did others experience it exactly the way I did? If the answers are all yes, then why are all these kinds of experiences understood uniformly by everyone?

We can *never* answer that question by natural scientific analysis. Our experiences are what they are. The Trinity is like that. We see the way the Trinity "works," but we cannot work out the reason.

All three persons have *all* the characteristics in the Circle of Love. However, it is interesting that each person of God sometimes manifestly exhibits different aspects of his character. The Father sits on a throne whence justice is pronounced. The Son is pure mercy, the sacrificial lamb. He first loved us, and we love him in return. The Holy Spirit moves in our heart, nudging and guiding us. It is pointless to ask *why* God is this way. Like the blue sky, *he is what he is!*

We are fearfully and wonderfully made in the *image* of God. He made us male and female, and our individual lives are mysteriously bonded. Through marriage, we come to understand how God binds himself to us in the person of Jesus Christ.

Why does God love us? This *is* answerable. It is not because he gives love—it is because God *is* love.

CHAPTER SEVEN

Three Days in Sheol

Jonah endured three days, and three nights in the belly of the great fish according to Scripture. Jesus told us that, like Jonah, he too would be in the bowels of the earth for three days. The three days is extremely important because *he* said it. If he lied, then he is not who he tells he is.

If, however, he told the truth, then there can be no doubt about who he is. Believing that he is who he said he was gets you through the door. There is much more.

Three Days Matter. God took six days for creation. Jesus was three days in *Sheol*.[1] He did not die on Good Friday as they taught me growing up.

Traditional Roman Catholic Easter celebrates Jesus, to the cheers of onlookers, entering Jerusalem triumphantly on Palm or Passion Sunday. He traveled along the road from Bethany westward across the Kidron Valley. That probably had him entering the city through the Eastern or Golden Gate.

Palm Sunday leads into Holy Monday and Holy Tuesday. Wednesday, also known as Holy Wednesday or Spy Wednesday, refers to Judas's betrayal. Tenebrae occurs on Spy Wednesday, and the clergy read a liturgy and gradually extinguish candles. Tenebrae is Latin for "shadows" or "darkness."

---

[1] Sheol: grave; by extension, realm of death, deepest depths. See John R. Kohlenberger, and James A. Swanson, *The Hebrew English Concordance to the Old Testament*, GK H8619.

Maundy Thursday commemorates the Last Supper. The Latin word means *mandatum* or *commandment*, reflecting Jesus's words, "I give you a new commandment." Good Friday commemorates the traditional day they crucified Jesus. Holy or Black Saturday is the day between his crucifixion and resurrection the following Sunday called Easter Day.

I'm not sure exactly how the church got mixed up about Passover week, but I think the confusion comes from the weekly Sabbath that starts at dusk on Friday, the last day of the week. The Passover is also a High Sabbath with the same restrictions, but the meal is very different.

Almost everyone seems curiously oblivious to the fact that there are only one and a half days between Good Friday and Easter Day. Jesus was very clear about how long he would be in the grave, and on more than one occasion.

Why is this important anyway? It is important because Jesus said it. If he was not dead for three days, then it leaves his credibility in doubt.

Jesus is the Almighty Son of God. If his words are true, then *all* the days of traditional Easter are wrong.

#

The Jewish Calendar. To understand the timeline of the Last Passover,[2] it is critical to understand some key differences between the Jewish and Gregorian calendar. Our day is from midnight to midnight while Jewish days are from dusk to dusk.

The modern day of the week, midnight to midnight, is not then completely analogous with the Jewish day of the week. In Genesis, God describes the evening and the morning as being a day, and gives them in that order. That is the reason for this discrepancy about when a day begins.

---

[2] The Last Passover here specifically refers to the Passover week when Jesus was crucified.

Look at this graphic of the Last Passover. The days of the week are shown along the top and the Jewish dates in large numerals along the bottom. Jewish days actually begin six hours before non-Jewish days. When you mix terms, then it can get confusing. You can see this from the image below. Look at Tuesday and 13 Nisan. They don't overlap precisely.

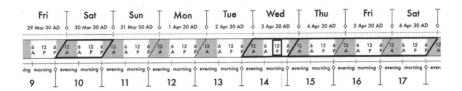

This can be most confusing when you mix the Jewish and non-Jewish understanding of what defines a "day." When I say *Tuesday 13 Nisan*, I am referring to the part of Tuesday which also overlaps on the Jewish day of 13 Nisan. That overlap between Tuesday and 13 Nisan is only eighteen hours instead of twenty-four. The last six hours of Tuesday from dusk to midnight is 14 Nisan, not 13 Nisan.

The Gregorian Calendar. In my discussions, ancient dates are Gregorian, not Julian, since that calendar is solar and Julian is not. In the graphic above, where you see the Gregorian date of 3 April AD 30, the Julian date is actually 5 April AD 30.[3]

Pope Gregory XIII instituted the Gregorian calendar in 1582. Purists may complain about the use of Gregorian dates before 1582, but in practice no one thinks of any prior date references as Julian dates. Probably many people never even knew there was a Julian calendar that predated the Gregorian.

Hour of the Day. For Romans and Jews, there were two different references to the hour of the day. For Romans, the first hour of the day was from 12 a.m. to 1 a.m. In the Jewish system, the first of the hour of the day began at 6 a.m. and ended at 7 a.m.

---

[3] Keisan Online Calculator. https://keisan.casio.com/exec/system/1227757509.

John uses the phrase "hour of the day"[4] in the Roman way, while the other synoptic Gospels and Acts use the Jewish meaning. So in John 19:13–14, he was referring to the sixth hour which ends at 6 a.m.

> [12] From then on Pilate sought to release him, but the Jews cried out, "If you release this man, you are not Caesar's friend. Everyone who makes himself a king opposes Caesar." [13] So when Pilate heard these words, he brought Jesus out and sat down on the judgment seat at a place called The Stone Pavement, and in Aramaic Gabbatha. [14] Now it was the day of Preparation of the Passover. It was about the sixth hour.[5] (John 19:12–13 ESV)

Watches. You will also sometime read about watches in Scripture. The following comes from the Scofield Study Bible Notes.[6]

Night (ancient)
First watch (Lam. 2:19) until about midnight.
Middle watch (Judg. 7:19) including midnight
(Ex. 11:4) until 3 a.m.

Night (New Testament)
First watch, evening = 6 to 9 p.m.
Second watch, midnight = 9 p.m. to 12 a.m.
Third watch, rooster-crow = 12 a.m. to 3 a.m.
Fourth watch, morning = 3 to 6 a.m.

Day (ancient)
Morning: until about 10 a.m.
Heat of the day: until about 2 p.m.
Day's decline: until about 6 p.m.
Evening or cool of the day: after 6 p.m.

The Calendar Year. The Jewish calendar is lunisolar which means it takes into account both the rotation of the moon and the sun. Other cultures, including Hindus and Buddhists as well as more than a half-dozen others, also use this kind of calendar.

---

[4] This is 6 a.m. John uses Roman time with the hours starting at 12 midnight and 12 noon, as is done today. However, the Synoptics use Hebrew calculations, beginning with sunrise (that is, 6 a.m.; 7 a.m. being the first hour, etc.). This is apparent from the care with which the Gospels which specify particular hours in relation to the crucifixion. Our Lord was put on the cross at 9 a.m. ("third hour" Mk. 15:25); darkness was over the land from noon until 3 p.m. ("sixth" till "ninth hour," Mt. 27:45–46; Mk. 15:33–34; Lk. 23:44). Thus here the "sixth hour" could not be Hebrew time (noon), but rather 6 a.m., "early in the morning" (Mt. 27:1–2). Acts uses Hebrew time. See Cyrus I. Scofield, and Doris W. Rikkers, eds. *The Scofield® Study Bible Notes*, John 19:14.
[5] The English Standard Version footnote for the sixth hour incorrectly states that this is noon.
[6] Cyrus I. Scofield, and Doris W. Rikkers, eds. *The Scofield® Study Bible Notes*. Gen. 1:5.

Jewish lunisolar calendars use both the phase of the moon and the time of the solar year and have an even number of months. This requires the calendar to have a thirteenth extra month every two or three years. These extra months are called *intercalary* or *embolismic* months. All lunisolar calendars require the addition of leap days, weeks, or months in some fashion.

Though the Gregorian calendars also requires a leap day, it is based only on the solar year of 365.25 days. Because the earth actually takes 365 days, 5 hours, 59 minutes and 16 seconds, or 365.2495 days to circle the sun, if you didn't add leap years, the calendar would gradually gain days and days over centuries. We even have to add a leap second to the calendar every year and a half or so in order to keep what we call UTC, or Coordinated Universal Time, in sync with astronomical time. Astronomical time is calculated from the cesium atom, which is more accurate even than the circumferential travel of earth around the sun.[7]

While leap years and leap seconds are not insignificant, they are not the most important thing to understand in this discussion. The difference between the Gregorian and Jewish calendar will become obvious as we continue.

The Jewish calendar has the following months starting with *Nisan* since God instituted the First Passover.[8]

Nisan (or Abib) = March–April
Iyyar (or Ziv) = April–May
Sivan = May–June
Tammuz = June–July
Ab = July–August
Elul = August–September
Tishri (or Ethanim) = September–October
Marchesvan (or Bul) = October–November
Kislev = November–December
Tebeth = December–January
Shebat = January–February
Adar = February–March

[7] National Institute of Standards and Technology. Leap Seconds FAQs, https://www.nist.gov/pml/time-and-frequency-division/leap-seconds-faqs.
[8] The First Passover refers to the initial Jewish Passover in Egypt.

Hebrew years differ from that of the Gregorian calendar. Maimonides wrote the *Mishneh Torah* in 1178 in which he placed the date of creation at the year 4938 A.M. on 3 Nisan. A.M. is the standard abbreviation for *anno mundi*,[9] which is Latin for "the year of the world." The word in Hebrew is לבריאת העולם, and it means "to the creation of the world."

In all my calendar dating work, I initially used the Macintosh® app called *Jewish Calendar* by Frank Yellin and Avi Drissman. Later, when they updated the app and years at the turn of the first century would not calculate, I began using a newer software called *Moadim*.[10] You can calculate the Hebrew year *before* Rosh Hashanah[11] (the Jewish civil new year) by adding 3760 to the Julian year. After Rosh Hashanah, you would add 3761.

⑧

The First Passover. The First Passover is *the* pattern for the Last Passover.

> [1] The LORD said to Moses and Aaron in the land of Egypt, [2] "This month shall be for you the beginning of months. It shall be the first month of the year for you. [3] Tell all the congregation of Israel that on the tenth day of this month every man shall take a lamb according to their fathers' houses, a lamb for a household. [4] And if the household is too small for a lamb, then he and his nearest neighbor shall take according to the number of persons; according to what each can eat you shall make your count for the lamb. [5] Your lamb shall be without blemish, a male a year old. You may take it from the sheep or from the goats, [6] and you shall keep it until the fourteenth day of this month, when the whole assembly of the congregation of Israel shall kill their lambs at twilight. (Ex. 12:1–6 ESV)

The First Passover in the month of Nisan is what I call the *figura umbra* of the Last Passover. The First Passover was so important that God directed the Hebrews to alter their calendar. This change is huge and signifies just how important Passover was.

---

9 A.M. abbrev. for *anno mundi*.

10 Safisoft, *Moadim*, https://apps.apple.com/us/app/moadim/id913651699?mt=12.

11 Chabad.org, "What Is Rosh Hashanah?" https://www.chabad.org/library/article_cdo/aid/4762/jewish/What-Is-Rosh-Hashanah.htm.

Equally important is 10 Nisan. Why would God choose that day to bring a spotless lamb into the house that, in a few short days, would be slaughtered and eaten? This unblemished lamb was quite literally set apart from the rest of the sheep. Each household took one and only *one lamb*. This point will have great importance, as you will see.

The verb "take" in verse 3 translates this way in the Kohlenberger/Mounce Hebrew dictionary. Note how that one form can also carry the sense of taking a wife in marriage. This will also be important. To get greater understanding of Hebrew verb tenses shown in bold abbreviation here, see the *Appendix* article entitled *A Guide to Kohlenberger/Mounce References.*

> **GK H4374 | S H3947** לָקַח *lāqaḥ* 967x
> v. [root of: 4375, 4376, 4917, 4918?, 4920, 5228, 5229]. **Q** to take, receive; **Qp** to be led away; **N** to be captured, taken away; **Pu** to be taken away, brought; **Ht** to flash back and forth; by extension: to gain possession, exercise authority; "to take a woman" means "to marry a wife". » accept; capture; choose; deprive; get; grasp; marry; receive; seize; take.

The end of 14 Nisan, at dusk, i.e., the beginning of 15 Nisan, designates the beginning of Passover. All the lambs or goats are killed at the same time, and all are roasted over fire. It was all consumed and anything left is completely burned.

Scripture calls 14 Nisan the Day of Preparation of Passover. Passover on 15 Nisan is also the first day of the Feast of Unleavened Bread. Because they prepared the food for Passover the day before, Jewish observers removed all leaven from their home on 14 Nisan and called it the Day of Preparation of Passover. This prevents any leaven making its way into the Passover meal by accident. Bear this in mind so you do not become confused. Scripture says that the Feast of Unleavened Bread begins on Passover and is seven days. Various Jewish locales included the Day of Preparation of Passover, however, so their feast lasted eight days.

[14] "This day shall be for you a memorial day, and you shall keep it as a feast to the LORD; throughout your generations, as a statute forever, you shall keep it as a feast. [15] Seven days you shall eat unleavened bread.

On the first day you shall remove leaven out of your houses, for if anyone eats what is leavened, from the first day until the seventh day, that person shall be cut off from Israel. [16] On the first day you shall hold a holy assembly, and on the seventh day a holy assembly. No work shall be done on those days. But what everyone needs to eat, that alone may be prepared by you.

[17] And you shall observe the Feast of Unleavened Bread, for on this very day I brought your hosts out of the land of Egypt. Therefore you shall observe this day, throughout your generations, as a statute forever. [18] In the first month, from the fourteenth day of the month at evening, you shall eat unleavened bread until the twenty-first day of the month at evening. [19] For seven days no leaven is to be found in your houses. If anyone eats what is leavened, that person will be cut off from the congregation of Israel, whether he is a sojourner or a native of the land. [20] You shall eat nothing leavened; in all your dwelling places you shall eat unleavened bread." (Ex. 12:14–20 ESV)

Scripture equates leaven to sin because it permeates the whole of the bread just as sin pervades the whole person. Sin is not just crossing the line—it aberrates truth. God is never anything but truthful. Because his is always truthful, he requires nothing less for the creation that he loves. Sin is brutal, and it ultimately kills us.

[56] The sting of death is sin… (1 Cor. 15:56 ESV)

#

Aligning the Days. There are three key factors that pin all the other events down.

Because we don't know the day of the First Passover, we cannot determine for certainty if the same specific day of week for the First Passover and the Last Passover both aligned within the Hebrew calendar. From year to year, the day of the week on which 14 Nisan falls can vary. Passover can fall on a Monday, Wednesday, Friday, or Saturday, but *never* on a Tuesday or Thursday!

Remember that Passover does not begin until dusk on Wednesday, when 14 Nisan *ends* and 15 Nisan *begins*. Scripture refers to 14 Nisan as the Day of Preparation of Passover. It begins a full twenty-four hours before Passover. Unless you carefully read the context of surrounding verses, the Day of Preparation of Passover can easily be mistaken for Passover.

These last two of those three key factors precisely align the Last Passover; *Jesus must be killed and dead in the grave for three days, and Passover never occurs on a Tuesday or Thursday.* It turns out that Wednesday, 15 Nisan Passover is the only day that will fit for the Day of Preparation of Passover and thus allow Jesus to be in the grave for three full days.

Only Mark 11:11 records the first factor, but it dovetails with the last two and squarely nails down all the other days of the week of the Last Passover. We traditionally refer to Palm Sunday as the day Jesus entered Jerusalem. It actually occurred on Saturday morning, the day of the weekly Sabbath, and not Sunday. That day was also 10 Nisan, as described in Exodus when all the lambs are taken into the household.

On 10 Nisan of the Last Passover, Jesus is being hailed on the road from Bethany with palm branches. We focus on this "triumphant entry" rather than the fact that he is actually going into Jerusalem to do *one* thing. He is going to the Temple to fulfill the Scripture. When he arrives, no one is there though because it is the weekly Sabbath. Jesus, the Lamb of God and the ultimate sacrifice, presents himself alone in his Father's *house* in accordance with Exodus 12:3. Though the crowds lauding him along the way also fulfill Scripture, they are oblivious. Their praise is not why Jesus went to the Temple.

> [11] And he entered Jerusalem and went into the temple. And when he had looked around at everything, as it was already late, he went out to Bethany with the twelve. (Mark 11:11 ESV)

We know this was indeed the Sabbath because the Temple was deserted and silent. The next day is Sunday, the first day of the Passover week. We easily get confused because for us today, it is the day of rest, but for the Jews then, it was like our busy Monday.

Commercial activity breaks the Temple silence as described in Mark 11:15. The din comes from merchants selling sacrifice animals and money-changers serving Jews coming from all over Judea for Passover.

Money-changers used stones with various weights standardized on the shekel so that visitors could buy animals for the Passover sacrifice from the merchants. In a practical way, these services were important to those coming from outside Jerusalem who did not bring a sacrifice animal along. But the Temple was not the place for all this, and the chief priests who allowed it were no doubt taking their portion of profits from livestock sales and money-changing fees.

Those three elements together firmly affix the events of the Last Passover and put Jesus on the road, arriving in Bethany some six days before. They are traveling on 8 Nisan and arrive at the house of Mary, Martha, and Lazarus as dusk and 9 Nisan arrives. Remember that Wednesday morning, 14 Nisan, the Romans nail Jesus to a cross and friends place him in a tomb by sunset just before Passover emerges on 15 Nisan.

One last point is key. The Last Supper and the Last Passover are *not* the same. The Last Supper, i.e., the Day of Preparation of Passover, is the day *before* the Last Passover. After the Last Supper, the chief priests arrest Jesus in Gethsemane and take him first to Caiaphas, the chief priest, and then on to Pilate. John records the following.

> [28] Then they led Jesus from the house of Caiaphas to the governor's headquarters. It was early morning. <u>They themselves did not enter the governor's headquarters, so that they would not be defiled, but could eat the Passover</u>. [29] So Pilate went outside to them and said, "What accusation do you bring against this man?" (John 18:28–29 ESV)

Jesus had already broken bread and shared wine at the Last Supper before arrest. Here John notes that the chief priests would not enter Pilate's headquarters because they would be ceremonially defiled. They could not then partake of the Passover—which means they had not yet had Passover. They would *not* have gone to see Pilate on Passover because it was a High Sabbath.

CHAPTER EIGHT

Bride-Price and Blood Token

Thursday and Friday, 8–9 Nisan 3790. The story of the Last Passover begins on 8 Nisan 3790 A.M.

The Last Passover Nisan 3790

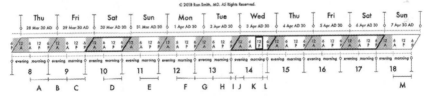

The Last Passover Timeline Bookmark.

[1] Six days before the Passover, Jesus therefore came to Bethany, where Lazarus was, whom Jesus had raised from the dead. [2] So they gave a dinner for him there. Martha served, and Lazarus was one of those reclining with him at table. [3] Mary therefore took a pound of expensive ointment made from pure nard, and anointed the feet of Jesus and wiped his feet with her hair. The house was filled with the fragrance of the perfume. [4] But Judas Iscariot, one of his disciples (he who was about to betray him), said, [5] "Why was this ointment not sold for three hundred denarii and given to the poor?" [6] He said this, not because he cared about the poor, but because he was a thief, and having charge of the moneybag he used to help himself to what was put into it. [7] Jesus said, "Leave her alone, so that she may keep it for the day of my burial. [8] For the poor you always have with you, but you do not always have me." (John 12:1–8 ESV)

On my visit to Israel, we learned that most cities are no more than about 28 miles apart. This is about the distance that one can walk in a day. Jesus and his disciples are traveling during the day on Thursday, 8 Nisan, and reach the house of Mary, Martha, and Lazarus around dusk as Friday, 9 Nisan begins. Remember, to non-Jewish people, this would be Thursday evening.

Sabbath does not begin till the end of the next day, Friday, again at dusk. The meal they are eating here is not a weekly Sabbath meal.

From his perspective, Mark records a flashback which aligns to this event in John. It further details that the honorary meal occurred at the house of Simon, the Leper. It suggests that Jesus's coming to Bethany and Jerusalem was absolutely intentional. It would have been planned for many days and thus widely noised about.

You will notice in Mark, that Jesus made a specific reference that the anointing was for his burial. He knows that he is coming for the Last Passover. The anointing oil is not a *mikvah*, which is always water.

> [3] And while he was at Bethany in the house of Simon the leper, as he was reclining at table, a woman came with an alabaster flask of ointment of pure nard, very costly, and she broke the flask and poured it over his head. [4] There were some who said to themselves indignantly, "Why was the ointment wasted like that? [5] For this ointment could have been sold for more than three hundred denarii and given to the poor." And they scolded her. [6] But Jesus said, "Leave her alone. Why do you trouble her? She has done a beautiful thing to me. [7] For you always have the poor with you, and whenever you want, you can do good for them.
> But you will not always have me. [8] She has done what she could; she has anointed my body beforehand for burial.
> [9] And truly, I say to you, wherever the gospel is proclaimed in the whole world, what she has done will be told in memory of her." (Mark 14:3–9 ESV)

John recounts the events of Friday, 9 Nisan. News had long spread among the people about Jesus after he raised Lazarus from the dead. The crowd he encountered would be expected because everyone knew Jesus was coming. Many of them were there, hoping to see another miracle.

> [9] When the sizeable crowd of the Jews learned that Jesus was there, they came, not only on account of him but also to see Lazarus, whom he had raised from the dead. [10] So the chief priests made plans to put Lazarus to death as well, [11] because on account of him many of the Jews were going away and believing in Jesus. (John 12:9–11 ESV)

Why did Jesus stay with Lazarus, Mary, and Martha? The raising of Lazarus from the dead is certainly fresh on everyone's mind. But it will be foremost in everyone's mind with the events of 14 Nisan and then 18 Nisan.

⚛

Saturday, 10 Nisan 3790. This day will mark the first event that pins the other Last Passover events to their specific days of the week.

Remember from Exodus 12:3, that on 10 Nisan of the First Passover everyone was to take a lamb to their household. Whether that was in the living area of their house, or in a room attached to it, we are not sure. Historically, they brought animals into either of those places according to Tim Chaffey[1] who wrote about Jesus's own birthplace in Bethlehem.

Wherever they kept the lamb, the significance of Exodus 12:3 cannot be understated. While Jesus was being cheered along the road from Bethany, many sheep and goats were entering Jerusalem through the Sheep Gate on that same day to comply with Exodus 12:3.

As detailed in Matthew 21:1–7, that ride into Jerusalem and on a never-before-ridden donkey fulfills Zechariah 9:9. Most people don't seem to be aware of the sheer numbers of animals coming into the city that same day for the same purpose. Scripture required the taking of animals on 10 Nisan for roasting on Passover, and Jews from everywhere converged on Jerusalem by routine.

> [9]   Rejoice greatly, O daughter of Zion!
>   Shout aloud, O daughter of Jerusalem!

---

[1] Tim Chaffey. "Born in a Barn (Stable)?" *Answers in Genesis*, https://answersingenesis.org/holidays/christmas/born-in-a-barn-stable/.

Behold, your king is coming to you;
  righteous and having salvation is he,
humble and mounted on a donkey,
  on a colt, the foal of a donkey.
(Zech. 9:9 ESV)

[12] The next day the large crowd that had come to the feast heard that Jesus was coming to Jerusalem. [13] So they took branches of palm trees and went out to meet him, crying out, "Hosanna! Blessed is he who comes in the name of the Lord, even the King of Israel!" [14] And Jesus found a young donkey and sat on it, just as it is written,
[15] "Fear not, daughter of Zion;
  behold, your king is coming,
    sitting on a donkey's colt!"
[16] His disciples did not understand these things at first, but when Jesus was glorified, then they remembered that these things had been written about him and had been done to him. [17] The crowd that had been with him when he called Lazarus out of the tomb and raised him from the dead continued to bear witness. [18] The reason why the crowd went to meet him was that they heard he had done this sign. (John 12:12–18 ESV)

Though the roadside crowd who witnessed or knew about Jesus raising Lazarus cheers him on, they have their own expectations. It seems clear from other places in Scripture that many were probably expecting a military king who was going to relieve them of Roman domination. However, riding in on a donkey is not the way a conqueror comes into a vanquished city.

What happens after Jesus enters Jerusalem, probably through the Golden Gate, holds the real significance to this day. The Golden Gate is visible today from the Mount of Olives across the Kidron Valley, though Ottoman Sultan Suleiman sealed it off with stone in 1541. Also known as the Eastern Gate, or *Sha'ar HaRachamimi*, the Hebrew means "Gate of Mercy." Bethany, which is traditionally identified as the present day West Bank city of Al-Eizariya, means in Arabic *Place of Lazarus*. This is also the site of the reputed Tomb of Lazarus.

Bethany is located about 1.5 miles, or 2.4 km, to the east of Jerusalem on the south-eastern slope of the Mount of Olives. The fact that it was within the approximate two-mile walk meant that walking from Bethany to Jerusalem was permitted on the Sabbath is important here. Jesus would not break his own commandments to rest on the Sabbath, and he did not do so when he went to Jerusalem.

What happens along the way fulfills prophecy. However, it is what Jesus did after he entered through that gate which fulfills his own commandment in Exodus 12:3. There is but one Scripture I've found which mentions this, and it bears repeating.

> [11] And he entered Jerusalem and went into the temple. And when he had looked around at everything, as it was already late, he went out to Bethany with the twelve. (Mark 11:11 ESV)

It could have been enough that Jesus simply entered the city, but it is much more significant that he goes into the Temple itself. Because 10 Nisan is Sabbath, there is no one there as would otherwise have been the case. Mark tells us that Jesus went into an *empty* Temple.

According to *his* own words in Exodus, Jesus presents himself in the Temple, the *house* of God, as *the* Last Passover lamb. The whole of the first Passover instructions are a precise portend of the Last Passover from its beginning to end.

God has just fulfilled Abraham's prophetic words in Genesis. He will provide *himself* as the last sacrifice. Moreover, the place that God took Abraham *is* Mount Moriah, where the Temple Mount is today.

> [1] After these things God tested Abraham and said to him, "Abraham!" And he said, "Here I am."
> [2] He said, "Take your son, your only son Isaac, whom you love, and go to the land of Moriah, and offer him there as a burnt offering on one of the mountains of which I shall tell you."
> [3] So Abraham rose early in the morning, saddled his donkey, and took two of his young men with him, and his son Isaac. And he cut the wood for the burnt offering and arose and went to the place of which God had told him.
> [4] On the third day Abraham lifted up his eyes and saw the place from afar. [5] Then Abraham said to his young men, "Stay here with the donkey;

I and the boy will go over there and worship and come again to you."
⁶ And Abraham took the wood of the burnt offering and laid it on Isaac his son. And he took in his hand the fire and the knife. So they went both of them together. ⁷ And Isaac said to his father Abraham, "My father!" And he said, "Here I am, my son." He said, "Behold, the fire and the wood, but where is the lamb for a burnt offering?"
⁸ Abraham said, "God will provide for *himself* the lamb for a burnt offering, my son." So they went both of them together.
⁹ When they came to the place of which God had told him, Abraham built the altar there and laid the wood in order and bound Isaac his son and laid him on the altar, on top of the wood. ¹⁰ Then Abraham reached out his hand and took the knife to slaughter his son.
¹¹ But the angel of the LORD called to him from heaven and said, "Abraham, Abraham!" And he said, "Here I am." ¹² He said, "Do not lay your hand on the boy or do anything to him, for now I know that you fear God, seeing you have not withheld your son, your only son, from me."
¹³ And Abraham lifted up his eyes and looked, and behold, behind him was a ram, caught in a thicket by his horns. And Abraham went and took the ram and offered it up as a burnt offering instead of his son.
¹⁴ So Abraham called the name of that place, "The LORD will provide"; as it is said to this day, "On the mount of the LORD it shall be provided." (Gen. 22:1–14 ESV)

Genesis here is also a *figura umbra* of the Last Passover. Jesus is the substitute sacrifice, like the ram caught in the bush. He is at Temple, which *is* Mount Moriah, on 10 Nisan for no other reason than to say to his Father that he is *in* the house of God.

His presence declares, "I AM the Lamb of God."

⌗

Sunday, 11 Nisan 3790. There are three important things that happen on this day. All of them are related and linked.

Unlike the previous day, the Temple is very, very busy. How à propos it is that Jesus presents himself to his Father in the Temple in the presence of only his disciples. Any other day, the significance of 10 Nisan would have been overshadowed. Instead of the quiet Temple of Sabbath, he finds profane busyness has beset the House of God. Prophetic Scripture sums up the emotion he was feeling.

⁷ For it is for your sake that I have borne reproach,
    that dishonor has covered my face.
⁸ I have become a stranger to my brothers,
    an alien to my mother's sons.
⁹ *For zeal for your house has consumed me,*
    and the reproaches of those who reproach you have fallen on me.
(Ps. 69:7–9 ESV)

The first of the three things was the encounter with the fig tree. The link between the fig tree and what Israel has become are unmistakable. The fig tree *is* the *figura umbra* of Israel.

¹² On the following day, when they came from Bethany, he was hungry. ¹³ And seeing in the distance a fig tree in leaf, he went to see if he could find anything on it. When he came to it, he found nothing but leaves, for it was not the season for figs.
¹⁴ And he said to it, "May no one ever eat fruit from you again." And his disciples heard it.
¹⁵ And they came to Jerusalem. And he entered the temple and began to drive out those who sold and those who bought in the temple, and he overturned the tables of the money-changers and the seats of those who sold pigeons. ¹⁶ And he would not allow anyone to carry anything through the temple.
¹⁷ And he was teaching them and saying to them, "Is it not written, 'My house shall be called a house of prayer for all the nations'? But you have made it a den of robbers."
¹⁸ And the chief priests and the scribes heard it and were seeking a way to destroy him, for they feared him, because all the crowd was astonished at his teaching. ¹⁹ And when evening came they went out of the city.
²⁰ As they passed by in the morning, they saw the fig tree withered away to its roots. ²¹ And Peter remembered and said to him, "Rabbi, look! The fig tree that you cursed has withered." (Mark 11:12–21 ESV)

Israel was chosen by God to be a witness to the world, but like the fig tree, they were no longer bearing fruit. Reading Jeremiah and Hosea alongside Mark and Matthew is a bit chilling.

¹¹ They have healed the wound of my people lightly,
    saying, 'Peace, peace,'
    when there is no peace.
¹² Were they ashamed when they committed abomination?
    No, they were not at all ashamed;

they did not know how to blush.
Therefore they shall fall among the fallen;
when I punish them, they shall be overthrown,
says the LORD.
¹³ When I would gather them, declares the LORD,
there are no grapes on the vine,
nor figs on the fig tree;
even the leaves are withered,
and what I gave them has passed away from them."
(Jer. 8:11–13 ESV)

¹⁰ Like grapes in the wilderness,
I found Israel.
Like the first fruit on the fig tree
in its first season,
I saw your fathers.
But they came to Baal-peor²
and consecrated themselves to the thing of shame,
and became detestable like the thing they loved.
¹¹ Ephraim's glory shall fly away like a bird—
no birth, no pregnancy, no conception!
¹² Even if they bring up children,
I will bereave them till none is left.
Woe to them
when I depart from them!
(Hos. 9:10–12 ESV)

The second significant thing occurred on the Mount of Olives when Jesus told the parable about a vineyard. It is curious that vineyards grow grapes, not figs. Why is the fig tree planted in this vineyard?

⁶ And he told this parable: "A man had a fig tree planted in his vineyard, and he came seeking fruit on it and found none. ⁷ And he said to the vinedresser, 'Look, for three years now I have come seeking fruit on this fig tree, and I find none. Cut it down. Why should it use up the ground?'
⁸ And he answered him, 'Sir, let it alone this year also, until I dig around it and put on manure. ⁹ Then if it should bear fruit next year, well and good; but if not, you can cut it down.'" (Luke 13:6–9 ESV)

² Numbers 21:1-5. At Mount Peor, the Israelites offered sacrifices to the dead and participated in orgies with Moabite women.

For over three years Jesus has been "digging around the fig tree" and still there is no fruit. This is prophetic because time has run out for Israel's witness.

The fig tree is even more significant when you look at this prophetic verse below in both the English Standard Version and the Amplified Bible. There are two staffs. One is for tribal identity and the other for judicial authority.

By the time of the Last Passover, Israel has already lost judicial authority. Just forty short years later, Rome destroyed the Temple and scattered Israel. Jewish tribal identity was lost forever, as Genesis prophesied.[3] All this caused the Lord such sadness and anger that day. Psalm 69 gives insight into his thoughts.

> [6] Let not those who hope in you be put to shame through me,
>   O Lord GOD of hosts;
>   let not those who seek you be brought to dishonor through me,
>   O God of Israel.
> [7] For it is for your sake that I have borne reproach,
>   that dishonor has covered my face.
> [8] I have become a stranger to my brothers,
>   an alien to my mother's sons.
> [9] For zeal for your house has consumed me,
>   and the reproaches of those who reproach you have fallen on me.
> [10] When I wept and humbled my soul with fasting,
>   it became my reproach.
> [11] When I made sackcloth my clothing,
>   I became a byword to them.
> [12] I am the talk of those who sit in the gate,
>   and the drunkards make songs about me.
>   (Ps. 69:6–12 ESV)

The third significant thing happens when they arrive at the Temple. His love and zeal for his Father's House prompts Jesus to drive out those who have commercialized it.

> [48] And when he drew near and saw the city, he wept over it, [42] saying, "Would that you, even you, had known on this day the things that make for peace! But now they are hidden from your eyes. [43] For the days will come upon you, when your enemies will set up a barricade around you

---

[3] Michael Rydelnik, *My Search for Messiah.*

and surround you and hem you in on every side [44] and tear you down to the ground, you and your children within you. And they will not leave one stone upon another in you, because you did not know the time of your visitation."

[45] And he entered the temple and began to drive out those who sold, [46] saying to them, "It is written, 'My house shall be a house of prayer,' but you have made it a den of robbers."

[47] And he was teaching daily in the temple. The chief priests and the scribes and the principal men of the people were seeking to destroy him, [48] but they did not find anything they could do, for all the people were hanging on his words. (Luke 19:41–48 ESV)

⧻

Monday, 12 Nisan 3790. The previous day, Jesus drove out the sellers of sacrifice animals and the money-changers. The Pharisees and scribes are stunned. Nothing like that had ever happened before. There are now just two days until the Last Passover.

Jesus and his disciples again trek from Bethany to the Temple across the Mount of Olives. As they walk by the fig tree, the disciples are astonished to find it now withered.[4]

Jesus explains that it takes faith. But it is not faith in any "name it claim it" way that we hear today. Jesus does not teach the disciples to command God. He has taught them that he does only what he sees the Father do. He trusts what the Father tells and shows him. That is the kind of faith he is talking about. He saw the Father do it and he did it. The withering of the fig is prophetic.

> [20] As they passed by in the morning, they saw the fig tree withered away to its roots. [21] And Peter remembered and said to him, "Rabbi, look! The fig tree that you cursed has withered." [22] And Jesus answered them, "Have faith in God. [23] Truly, I say to you, whoever says to this mountain, 'Be taken up and thrown into the sea,' and does not doubt in his heart, but believes that what he says will come to pass, it will be done for him. [24] Therefore I tell you, whatever you ask in prayer, believe that you have received it, and it will be yours. [25] And whenever you stand praying, forgive, if you have anything against anyone, so that your Father also who is in heaven may forgive you your trespasses." (Mark 11:20–25 ESV)

---

[4] Ron Smith, *Between Justice and Mercy.* See Mark 11:12-14 in "Sunday, 11 Nisan 3790."

Continuing on, they finally reach the Temple. Mark records at least a half-dozen of Jesus's parables. Jesus knows that his time is very close. He is ready, and he is making this day count.

Before he begins teaching, he first deals with the chief priests, scribes, and elders who challenge him. They are angry, but they are also without any reply. With the sellers and money-changers gone, the source of their income is now gone. They could only take their cut if the selling and money-changing was happening there in the Temple.

Even worse, they have lost face with all the people. They are caught between the people and the Roman occupiers who want social stability in Jerusalem. Nothing like that had happened before, and the seriousness of the situation for them is critical.

> [12] And they came again to Jerusalem. And as he was walking in the temple, the chief priests and the scribes and the elders came to him, [28] and they said to him, "By what authority are you doing these things, or who gave you this authority to do them?"
> [29] Jesus said to them, "I will ask you one question; answer me, and I will tell you by what authority I do these things. [30] Was the baptism of John from heaven or from man? Answer me."
> [31] And they discussed it with one another, saying, "If we say, 'From heaven,' he will say, 'Why then did you not believe him?' [32] But shall we say, 'From man'?"—they were afraid of the people, for they all held that John really was a prophet. [33] So they answered Jesus, "We do not know." And Jesus said to them, "Neither will I tell you by what authority I do these things." (Mark 11:27–33 ESV)

The wisdom of men is no match for the wisdom of God. Now silenced, the chief priests are backed into a desperate corner. The only way to rescue themselves and restore their livelihood is to be rid of Jesus.

Following his rebuke, the first of series of parables recorded by Mark shows that Jesus clearly knows what they are thinking. I'm sure the chief priests knew exactly what Jesus was saying. His rebuke is like throwing gasoline onto a fire. Israel is bearing no more fruit. Like the fig tree, it will wither.

¹ And he began to speak to them in parables. "A man planted a vineyard and put a fence around it and dug a pit for the winepress and built a tower, and leased it to tenants and went into another country.
² When the season came, he sent a servant to the tenants to get from them some of the fruit of the vineyard. ³ And they took him and beat him and sent him away empty-handed.
⁴ Again he sent to them another servant, and they struck him on the head and treated him shamefully. ⁵ And he sent another, and him they killed. And so with many others: some they beat, and some they killed.
⁶ He had still one other, a beloved son. Finally he sent him to them, saying, 'They will respect my son.'
⁷ But those tenants said to one another, 'This is the heir. Come, let us kill him, and the inheritance will be ours.' ⁸ And they took him and killed him and threw him out of the vineyard.
⁹ What will the owner of the vineyard do? He will come and destroy the tenants and give the vineyard to others. ¹⁰ Have you not read this Scripture:

" 'The stone that the builders rejected

   has become the cornerstone;
¹¹   this was the Lord's doing,

   and it is marvelous in our eyes?'"
¹² And they were seeking to arrest him but feared the people, for they perceived that he had told the parable against them. So they left him and went away. (Mark 12:1–12 ESV)

Put to shame, the chief priests will try to trap Jesus. To challenge him, they send other Pharisees along with the politicians under Herod Antipas. Herod Antipas is the son of Herod the Great and also governor over Galilee and Perea. No doubt Herod Antipas is getting his cut of the trade on the Temple Mount as well. He likely has a vested financial interest in seeing Jesus gone as well.

The chief priests take a new tack by bringing Roman power to bear, but the wisdom of God wins again.

¹³ And they sent to him some of the Pharisees and some of the Herodians, to trap him in his talk. ¹⁴ And they came and said to him, "Teacher, we know that you are true and do not care about anyone's opinion. For you are not swayed by appearances, but truly teach the way of God. Is it lawful to pay taxes to Caesar, or not? Should we pay them, or should we not?" ¹⁵ But, knowing their hypocrisy, he said to them,

"Why put me to the test? Bring me a denarius and let me look at it."
[16] And they brought one. And he said to them, "Whose likeness and inscription is this?" They said to him, "Caesar's."
[17] Jesus said to them, "Render to Caesar the things that are Caesar's, and to God the things that are God's." And they marveled at him. (Mark 12:13–17 ESV)

The Sadducees then take their shot at Jesus. They were a powerful minority of the religious leaders in the Sanhedrin. Sadducees differed from Pharisees in that they only recognized the first five books of Moses as sacred. For that reason, they refused to believe in the resurrection, among other things.

That is why they try to assault the belief in the resurrection using the Scripture from Deuteronomy 25:5–6. There it speaks of sons living in the close proximity of a household. This was not simply a family relationship, but an economic one as well. That is why it was the obligation of the younger brothers to raise up children to the older married brother if he died childless.

The trap is ingenious, but once again, the wisdom of God shuts them down.

[18] And Sadducees came to him, who say that there is no resurrection. And they asked him a question, saying, [19] "Teacher, Moses wrote for us that if a man's brother dies and leaves a wife, but leaves no child, the man must take the widow and raise up offspring for his brother.
[20] There were seven brothers; the first took a wife, and when he died left no offspring. [21] And the second took her, and died, leaving no offspring. And the third likewise. [22] And the seven left no offspring. Last of all the woman also died. [23] In the resurrection, when they rise again, whose wife will she be? For the seven had her as wife."
[24] Jesus said to them, "Is this not the reason you are wrong, because you know neither the Scriptures nor the power of God? [25] For when they rise from the dead, they neither marry nor are given in marriage, but are like angels in heaven. [26] And as for the dead being raised, have you not read in the book of Moses, in the passage about the bush, how God spoke to him, saying, 'I am the God of Abraham, and the God of Isaac, and the God of Jacob'?
[27] He is not God of the dead, but of the living. You are quite wrong." (Mark 12:18–27 ESV)

Jesus is seeing hearts changed even in the Sanhedrin. That is what he yearns for. Mark documents this next in his narrative, which clearly points back to the God's primary characteristic of agape love.

[28] And one of the scribes came up and heard them disputing with one another, and seeing that he answered them well, asked him, "Which commandment is the most important of all?" [29] Jesus answered, "The most important is, 'Hear, O Israel: The Lord our God, the Lord is one. [30] And you shall love the Lord your God with all your heart and with all your soul and with all your mind and with all your strength.' [31] The second is this: 'You shall love your neighbor as yourself.' There is no other commandment greater than these." [32] And the scribe said to him, "You are right, Teacher. You have truly said that he is one, and there is no other besides him. [33] And to love him with all the heart and with all the understanding and with all the strength, and to love one's neighbor as oneself, is much more than all whole burnt offerings and sacrifices." [34] And when Jesus saw that he answered wisely, he said to him, "You are not far from the kingdom of God." And after that no one dared to ask him any more questions. (Mark 12:28–34 ESV)

The assault from the religious leaders stops, but Jesus is not finished. He refers to Psalm 110 written by David, which refers to the Father and Son, two of the Trinity. In Mark 12:35, Jesus says that David was in the Holy Spirit. By doing so, he has just affirmed the Trinity, a word which is itself not in the Bible.

With no subtlety Jesus has just given them scriptural proof that the Son of God will be a son of David. They know what he is saying.

[35] And as Jesus taught in the temple, he said, "How can the scribes say that the Christ is the son of David? [36] David himself, in the Holy Spirit, declared,

" 'The Lord said to my Lord,

"Sit at my right hand,

until I put your enemies under your feet."'"

[37] David himself calls him Lord. So how is he his son?" And the great throng heard him gladly. (Mark 12:35–37 ESV)

Jesus then personally reproves them, the "religious." He affirms those who love God and demonstrates how they are proved. What is your treasure; your money or your God?

[38] And in his teaching he said, "Beware of the scribes, who like to walk around in long robes and like greetings in the marketplaces [39] and have the best seats in the synagogues and the places of honor at feasts, [40] who

devour widows' houses and for a pretense make long prayers. They will receive the greater condemnation."
[41] And he sat down opposite the treasury and watched the people putting money into the offering box. Many rich people put in large sums. [42] And a poor widow came and put in two small copper coins, which make a penny.
[43] And he called his disciples to him and said to them, "Truly, I say to you, this poor widow has put in more than all those who are contributing to the offering box. [44] For they all contributed out of their abundance, but she out of her poverty has put in everything she had, all she had to live on." (Mark 12:38–44 ESV)

This is a teaching moment for his disciples. They are leaving the Temple and walking back to Bethany across the Mount of Olives. He has been telling them he will be killed and rise again. The fate of the Temple is already set, and he knows what the disciples will face. He wants them to focus. In just two days they will be scattered momentarily. He is preparing them.

Jesus is not only speaking to what the disciples will experience. He is telling us today what to expect. The abomination of desolation in Daniel 9:27 will be repeated at the end of days. The fig tree again pops up. Israel, the fig tree, will come to life again. And so it was on May 14, 1948. The significance of the Nisan wedding feast is unmistakable. We will enjoy the marriage to our Savior.

[1] And as he came out of the temple, one of his disciples said to him, "Look, Teacher, what wonderful stones and what wonderful buildings!"
[2] And Jesus said to him, "Do you see these great buildings? There will not be left here one stone upon another that will not be thrown down."
[3] And as he sat on the Mount of Olives opposite the temple, Peter and James and John and Andrew asked him privately, [4] "Tell us, when will these things be, and what will be the sign when all these things are about to be accomplished?"
[5] And Jesus began to say to them, "See that no one leads you astray. [6] Many will come in my name, saying, 'I am he!' and they will lead many astray. [7] And when you hear of wars and rumors of wars, do not be alarmed. This must take place, but the end is not yet.
[8] For nation will rise against nation, and kingdom against kingdom. There will be earthquakes in various places; there will be famines. These are but the beginning of the birth pains.
[9] "But be on your guard. For they will deliver you over to councils, and you will be beaten in synagogues, and you will stand before governors

and kings for my sake, to bear witness before them. ¹⁰ And the gospel must first be proclaimed to all nations. ¹¹ And when they bring you to trial and deliver you over, do not be anxious beforehand what you are to say, but say whatever is given you in that hour, for it is not you who speak, but the Holy Spirit. ¹² And brother will deliver brother over to death, and the father his child, and children will rise against parents and have them put to death. ¹³ And you will be hated by all for my name's sake. But the one who endures to the end will be saved.

¹⁴ "But when you see the abomination of desolation standing where he ought not to be (let the reader understand), then let those who are in Judea flee to the mountains. ¹⁵ Let the one who is on the housetop not go down, nor enter his house, to take anything out, ¹⁶ and let the one who is in the field not turn back to take his cloak. ¹⁷ And alas for women who are pregnant and for those who are nursing infants in those days! ¹⁸ Pray that it may not happen in winter.

¹⁹ For in those days there will be such tribulation as has not been from the beginning of the creation that God created until now, and never will be. ²⁰ And if the Lord had not cut short the days, no human being would be saved. But for the sake of the elect, whom he chose, he shortened the days. ²¹ And then if anyone says to you, 'Look, here is the Christ!' or 'Look, there he is!' do not believe it. ²² For false christs and false prophets will arise and perform signs and wonders, to lead astray, if possible, the elect. ²³ But be on guard; I have told you all things beforehand.

²⁴ "But in those days, after that tribulation, the sun will be darkened, and the moon will not give its light, ²⁵ and the stars will be falling from heaven, and the powers in the heavens will be shaken. ²⁶ And then they will see the Son of Man coming in clouds with great power and glory. ²⁷ And then he will send out the angels and gather his elect from the four winds, from the ends of the earth to the ends of heaven.

²⁸ "From the fig tree learn its lesson: as soon as its branch becomes tender and puts out its leaves, you know that summer is near. ²⁹ So also, when you see these things taking place, you know that he is near, at the very gates. ³⁰ Truly, I say to you, this generation will not pass away until all these things take place. ³¹ Heaven and earth will pass away, but my words will not pass away.

³² "But concerning that day or that hour, no one knows, not even the angels in heaven, nor the Son, but only the Father. ³³ Be on guard, keep awake. For you do not know when the time will come. ³⁴ It is like a man going on a journey, when he leaves home and puts his servants in charge, each with his work, and commands the doorkeeper to stay awake. ³⁵ Therefore stay awake—for you do not know when the master of the house will come, in the evening, or at midnight, or when the rooster crows, or in the morning— ³⁶ lest he come suddenly and find you asleep. ³⁷ And what I say to you I say to all: Stay awake." (Mark 13:1–37 ESV)

Tuesday, 13 Nisan 3790. By this day, the chief priests have decided Jesus's fate and are making plans. He must die.

There are two important things happening in the daytime on 13 Nisan. The first thing was the discussion about making the arrangements for the Preparation of Passover. This occupies the disciples, who have only a handful of hours to complete the task. There is confusion about the Day of Preparation of Passover. Look at this in Mark and let me explain why I think this is.

> [12] And on the first day of Unleavened Bread, when they sacrificed the Passover lamb, his disciples said to him, "Where will you have us go and prepare for you to eat the Passover?" (Mark 14:12 ESV)

Notice that in this same passage we see "the first day of Unleavened Bread, when they sacrificed the Passover lamb" and also "prepare for you to eat the Passover." There are actually two different days being referred to here in this one Scripture.

The Day of Preparation of Passover begins at dusk as 13 Nisan ends and 14 Nisan begins. All leaven is removed from the home, and all the cooking, *except* for the roast lamb, is prepared. It is at dusk, i.e., twilight, when 14 Nisan fades into 15 Nisan, that the lambs are slain, and prepared and roasted over the fire as instructed in Exodus 12.

For some Jewish communities, the Feast of Unleavened Bread sometimes included the Day of Preparation of Passover. That means for those celebrants, it is traditionally eight days and not just seven. This appears to be a matter of local custom and does not affect the actual day of the Passover meal or the ending of the Feast of Unleavened bread.

This same confusion exists in both Matthew and Luke. They too support the idea that Day of Preparation of Passover may have been spoken of as the Passover, even though technically it was not.

> [17] Now on the first day of Unleavened Bread the disciples came to Jesus, saying, "Where will you have us prepare for you to eat the Passover?" [18] He said, "Go into the city to a certain man and say to him, 'The

Teacher says, My time is at hand. I will keep the Passover at your house with my disciples.'" [19] And the disciples did as Jesus had directed them, and they prepared the Passover. (Matt. 26:17–19 ESV)

[7] Then came the day of Unleavened Bread, on which the Passover lamb had to be sacrificed. [8] So Jesus sent Peter and John, saying, "Go and prepare the Passover for us, that we may eat it."
[9] They said to him, "Where will you have us prepare it?"
[10] He said to them, "Behold, when you have entered the city, a man carrying a jar of water will meet you. Follow him into the house that he enters [11] and tell the master of the house, 'The Teacher says to you, Where is the guest room, where I may eat the Passover with my disciples?' [12] And he will show you a large upper room furnished; prepare it there."
[13] And they went and found it just as he had told them, and they prepared the Passover. (Luke 22:7–13 ESV)

One last point of difference makes the distinction certain. At the Last Supper, i.e., the Day of Preparation of Passover, there is bread and wine. There is *no* roast lamb, which is center-stage at *all* Passover meals.

The instruction that every household must take a lamb on 10 Nisan is very specific, just as is the instruction to kill the lamb at dusk between 14 Nisan and 15 Nisan. Jesus died at 3 p.m. on 14 Nisan and was buried by dusk just as 15 Nisan started when all the other Passover lambs are being slain.

The second important thing is that Jesus's thorough rebuke of the chief priests the day before solidifies their plan to capture and kill him. Judas has become their misguided pawn in a full-blown conspiracy. While the rest of the disciples are making arrangements for the Day of Preparation of Passover, i.e., the Last Supper, Judas Iscariot has designs on how to identify and hand Jesus over to the chief priests.

The chief priests have foreseen a problem in trying to arrest Jesus during the day. The Jewish people love him, and they cannot risk a riot by taking him during the day. It must be done at night when everyone else is asleep. They also must involve the Roman named Pilate, since Israel did not have the authority to put him to death.

The timing is impeccable. The Last Supper occurs on the Day of Preparation of Passover. They plan the arrest for the middle of the night. The trial will be held very quickly before people even know they have arrested Jesus. They *must* involve Pilate in order to put Jesus to death. Israel would, with few exceptions, have stoned Jesus[5], not crucified him.

Romans executed prisoners by crucifixion. The Old Testament records a similar Hebrew fashion of death called "hanging on a tree." The execution itself was still usually by stoning and the body hanged for display.[6] It was not like Roman crucifixion which used nails to fasten the victim to the wood to produce a tortuous, prolonged, and asphyxiating death.

Judas's involvement with the chief priests is well documented.

> [1] It was now two days before the Passover and the Feast of Unleavened Bread. And the chief priests and the scribes were seeking how to arrest him by stealth and kill him, [2] for they said, "Not during the feast, lest there be an uproar from the people."…
> [10] Then Judas Iscariot, who was one of the twelve, went to the chief priests in order to betray him to them. [11] And when they heard it, they were glad and promised to give him money. And he sought an opportunity to betray him. (Mark 14:1–2, 10–11 ESV)

> [14] Then one of the twelve, whose name was Judas Iscariot, went to the chief priests [15] and said, "What will you give me if I deliver him over to you?" And they paid him thirty pieces of silver. [16] And from that moment he sought an opportunity to betray him. (Matt. 26:14–16 ESV)

> [1] Now the Feast of Unleavened Bread drew near, which is called the Passover. [2] And the chief priests and the scribes were seeking how to put him to death, for they feared the people. (Luke 22:1–2 ESV)

> [3] Then Satan entered into Judas called Iscariot, who was of the number of the twelve. [4] He went away and conferred with the chief priests and officers how he might betray him to them. [5] And they were glad, and agreed to give him money. [6] So he consented and sought an opportunity to betray him to them in the absence of a crowd. (Luke 22:3–6 ESV)

---

[5] My Jewish Learning, "The Death Penalty in Jewish Tradition" https://www.myjewishlearning.com/article/the-death-penalty-in-jewish-tradition/.
[6] Michael Rydelnik. *Moody Bible Commentary.*

CHAPTER NINE

The Last Passover

Wednesday, 14 Nisan 3790 and the Last Supper. The events of 14 Nisan begin as 13 Nisan fades with dusk and the evening ensues. Jesus and the disciples are in the upper room for the Day of Preparation of Passover, which is also known as the Fast of the Firstborn.[1] It is also where the disciples think they will celebrate Passover with Jesus the following evening. Many significant things are about to happen in short order.

Jewish houses often had upper rooms. During the daytime of 13 Nisan, Jesus is apparently in Bethany, not at the Temple. He tells Peter and John that they will see a man carrying a jar of water. By the way he instructs the disciples, it seems Jesus may have known the man already.

Remember from the last chapter they are going to *prepare* for Passover. This meal will not be a Passover meal with roast lamb. As I have shown, Mark writes, "the first day of Unleavened Bread, when they sacrificed the Passover lamb," which leads to this confusion. Recall also that the Day of Preparation of Passover requires all leaven be removed from the house, and that is why some celebrated an extra day as part of the Feast of Unleavened Bread.

Reading about specific events as recorded in the different Gospels without comparing one to another makes it easy to confuse the Day of Preparation of

---

[1] Wikipedia, "Fast of the Firstborn: When Passover begins after Shabbat," http://en.wikipedia.org/w/index.php?title=Fast_of_the_Firstborn&oldid=65098578.

Passover with Passover itself. They are tightly linked in the minds of the disciples and their narratives. Those who are not schooled in this feast's tradition can easily get the two confused.

Recall that leaven in any of the Passover meal represents sin and is forbidden, all food preparation was done prior to the beginning of Passover on 15 Nisan *except* the roast lamb. The lambs were killed at the *end* of 14 Nisan as 15 Nisan begins right before they were roasted and consumed entirely with all the other food.

> [17] Now on the first day of Unleavened Bread the disciples came to Jesus, saying, "Where will you have us prepare for you to eat the Passover?"
> [18] He said, "Go into the city to a certain man and say to him, 'The Teacher says, My time is at hand. I will keep the Passover at your house with my disciples.'"
> [19] And the disciples did as Jesus had directed them, and they prepared the Passover. [20] When it was evening, he reclined at table with the twelve. (Matt. 26:17–19 ESV)

> [12] And on the first day of Unleavened Bread, when they sacrificed the Passover lamb, his disciples said to him, "Where will you have us go and prepare for you to eat the Passover?"
> [13] And he sent two of his disciples and said to them, "Go into the city, and a man carrying a jar of water will meet you. Follow him, [14] and wherever he enters, say to the master of the house, 'The Teacher says, Where is my guest room, where I may eat the Passover with my disciples?' [15] And he will show you a large upper room furnished and ready; there prepare for us."
> [16] And the disciples set out and went to the city and found it just as he had told them, and they prepared the Passover. [17] And when it was evening, he came with the twelve. (Mark 14:12–18 ESV)

> [7] Then came the day of Unleavened Bread, on which the Passover lamb had to be sacrificed. [8] So Jesus sent Peter and John, saying, "Go and prepare the Passover for us, that we may eat it."
> [9] They said to him, "Where will you have us prepare it?"
> [10] He said to them, "Behold, when you have entered the city, a man carrying a jar of water will meet you. Follow him into the house that he enters [11] and tell the master of the house, 'The Teacher says to you, Where is the guest room, where I may eat the Passover with my disciples?'
> [12] And he will show you a large upper room furnished; prepare it there."
> [13] And they went and found it just as he had told them, and they

prepared the Passover. [14] And when the hour came, he reclined at table, and the apostles with him. (Luke 22:7–14 ESV)

Judas was already deep in the conspiracy to kill Jesus even before they share fellowship and an evening meal at the beginning of 14 Nisan, the Day of Preparation of Passover. It appears that Jesus did also wash Judas's feet and Jesus's own words in John suggest that he took of the bread and the wine. It would seem uncertain as to when Judas was possessed of Satan until you read the end of John 13.

[1] Now the Feast of Unleavened Bread drew near, which is called the Passover. [2] And the chief priests and the scribes were seeking how to put him to death, for they feared the people.
[3] Then Satan entered into Judas called Iscariot, who was of the number of the twelve. [4] He went away and conferred with the chief priests and officers how he might betray him to them. [5] And they were glad, and agreed to give him money. [6] So he consented and sought an opportunity to betray him to them in the absence of a crowd. (Luke 22:1–6 ESV)

[1] Now before the Feast of the Passover, when Jesus knew that his hour had come to depart out of this world to the Father, having loved his own who were in the world, he loved them to the end.
[2] During supper, when the devil had already put it into the heart of Judas Iscariot, Simon's son, to betray him, [3] Jesus, knowing that the Father had given all things into his hands, and that he had come from God and was going back to God, [4] rose from supper. He laid aside his outer garments, and taking a towel, tied it around his waist. [5] Then he poured water into a basin and began to wash the disciples' feet and to wipe them with the towel that was wrapped around him.
[6] He came to Simon Peter, who said to him, "Lord, do you wash my feet?" [7] Jesus answered him, "What I am doing you do not understand now, but afterward you will understand."
[8] Peter said to him, "You shall never wash my feet." Jesus answered him, "If I do not wash you, you have no share with me."
[9] Simon Peter said to him, "Lord, not my feet only but also my hands and my head!" [10] Jesus said to him, "The one who has bathed does not need to wash, except for his feet, but is completely clean. And you are clean, but not every one of you." [11] For he knew who was to betray him; that was why he said, "Not all of you are clean."
[12] When he had washed their feet and put on his outer garments and resumed his place, he said to them, "Do you understand what I have done to you? [13] You call me Teacher and Lord, and you are right, for so I am.
[14] If I then, your Lord and Teacher, have washed your feet, you also ought to wash one another's feet. [15] For I have given you an example,

that you also should do just as I have done to you. [16] Truly, truly, I say to you, a servant is not greater than his master, nor is a messenger greater than the one who sent him. [17] If you know these things, blessed are you if you do them. [18] I am not speaking of all of you; I know whom I have chosen. But the Scripture will be fulfilled, 'He who ate my bread has lifted his heel against me.' [19] I am telling you this now, before it takes place, that when it does take place you may believe that I am he. [20] Truly, truly, I say to you, whoever receives the one I send receives me, and whoever receives me receives the one who sent me." (John 13:1–20 ESV)

[17] Now on the first day of Unleavened Bread the disciples came to Jesus, saying, "Where will you have us prepare for you to eat the Passover?" [18] He said, "Go into the city to a certain man and say to him, 'The Teacher says, My time is at hand. I will keep the Passover at your house with my disciples.'" [19] And the disciples did as Jesus had directed them, and they prepared the Passover. [20] When it was evening, he reclined at table with the twelve. [21] And as they were eating, he said, "Truly, I say to you, one of you will betray me." [22] And they were very sorrowful and began to say to him one after another, "Is it I, Lord?" [23] He answered, "He who has dipped his hand in the dish with me will betray me. [24] The Son of Man goes as it is written of him, but woe to that man by whom the Son of Man is betrayed! It would have been better for that man if he had not been born." [25] Judas, who would betray him, answered, "Is it I, Rabbi?" He said to him, "You have said so." (Matt. 26:17–25 ESV)

The details here also tell us it was Peter who whispered to John sitting near him to ask Jesus who it was that would betray him. John whispered the question to Jesus who replied and then subtly handed the morsel to Judas. He then told Judas to do quickly what he intends. The disciples appear to be clueless because the interaction between Peter, John, and Jesus has been a whisper.

While Satan had put it into Judas Iscariot's heart to conspire with the chief priests to kill Jesus probably on 13 Nisan, it seems Satan entered him as soon as he took the dipped a morsel of bread. Judas whispers the rhetorical question, "Is it I, Rabbi?" not because he is undecided about the betrayal. Jesus's answer will tell Judas if he knows about the plan.

As soon as Jesus responds, Judas left before everyone there knows his scheme. Otherwise, why would the other disciples not have interrogated him further, or even tried to stop him? Recall that in just a few hours, Peter will lop off the ear of the chief priest's servant. He could fully deal with Judas.

Because Judas handled the money and he left abruptly, the other disciples think Jesus had instructed him to go buy something. He hid his plan well for the moment from the disciples.

> [21] After saying these things, Jesus was troubled in his spirit, and testified, "Truly, truly, I say to you, one of you will betray me." [22] The disciples looked at one another, uncertain of whom he spoke.
> [23] One of his disciples, whom Jesus loved, was reclining at table at Jesus' side, [24] so Simon Peter motioned to him to ask Jesus of whom he was speaking. [25] So that disciple, leaning back against Jesus, said to him, "Lord, who is it?"
> [26] Jesus answered, "It is he to whom I will give this morsel of bread when I have dipped it." So when he had dipped the morsel, he gave it to Judas, the son of Simon Iscariot.
> [27] Then after he had taken the morsel, Satan entered into him. Jesus said to him, "What you are going to do, do quickly."
> [28] Now no one at the table knew why he said this to him. [29] Some thought that, because Judas had the moneybag, Jesus was telling him, "Buy what we need for the feast," or that he should give something to the poor. [30] So, after receiving the morsel of bread, he immediately went out. And it was night. (John 13:21–30 ESV)

The Last Supper is analogous to the *erusin* of the ancient Jewish wedding.[2] The foot washing of the disciples by Jesus that evening is analogous to a ceremonial *mikvah* for the church. Jesus ceremonial cleansing had already occurred when he was anointed at Simon, the Leper's house.

The significance of the Last Supper is the sharing of the broken bread and the wine. The bread is the bride-price, and the broken bread is a *figura umbra* of Jesus's body. The wine is the symbol of our purity, like the *chuppah* cloth blood.

The Garden of Gethsemane. Judas had already departed. For the rest of the disciples, the ceremonial *erusin* was complete. Jesus tries to prepare them for

---

2 Ron Smith, *Between Justice and Mercy*, "How We Became the Bride of Christ."

his death on the cross and his absence for three days. He gives them a new commandment. It is the entire Ten Commandments framed this time, not in justice, but in agape love.

> [31] When he [Judas Iscariot] had gone out, Jesus said, "Now is the Son of Man glorified, and God is glorified in him. [32] If God is glorified in him, God will also glorify him in himself, and glorify him at once.
> [33] Little children, yet a little while I am with you. You will seek me, and just as I said to the Jews, so now I also say to you, 'Where I am going you cannot come.'
> [34] A new commandment I give to you, that you love one another: just as I have loved you, you also are to love one another. [35] By this all people will know that you are my disciples, if you have love for one another." (John 13:31–35 ESV)

Jesus and the remaining eleven disciples leave the upper room and go to Gethsemane. They would have to leave Jerusalem toward the Mount of Olives, where the garden was located. The moon was full, because the Jewish calendar is lunisolar, and it is now the middle of the month.

> [36] Then Jesus went with them to a place called Gethsemane, and he said to his disciples, "Sit here, while I go over there and pray." [37] And taking with him Peter and the two sons of Zebedee, he began to be sorrowful and troubled.
> [38] Then he said to them, "My soul is very sorrowful, even to death; remain here, and watch with me." [39] And going a little farther he fell on his face and prayed, saying, "My Father, if it be possible, let this cup pass from me; nevertheless, not as I will, but as you will."
> [40] And he came to the disciples and found them sleeping. And he said to Peter, "So, could you not watch with me one hour? [41] Watch and pray that you may not enter into temptation. The spirit indeed is willing, but the flesh is weak." [42] Again, for the second time, he went away and prayed, "My Father, if this cannot pass unless I drink it, your will be done." [43] And again he came and found them sleeping, for their eyes were heavy. [44] So, leaving them again, he went away and prayed for the third time, saying the same words again.
> [45] Then he came to the disciples and said to them, "Sleep and take your rest later on. See, the hour is at hand, and the Son of Man is betrayed into the hands of sinners. [46] Rise, let us be going; see, my betrayer is at hand." (Matt. 26:36–46 ESV)

Several things Jesus says here are very noteworthy. He says his "soul is very sorrowful." Yes, Jesus has a soul, just as we do. His soul and our soul are the essence of our person and personality. The soul is who we are. It is our life.

Jesus's life is timeless while also held in time by his body, while ours is eternal and God-breathed.

Our soul, i.e., our person, is what grieves. Why does God grieve? What *is* grief? Start with this in Genesis and let us see how the Hebrew words for repented and grieved translate.

> ⁵ And GOD saw that the wickedness of man was great in the earth, and that every imagination of the thoughts of his heart was only evil continually. ⁶ And it repented the LORD that he had made man on the earth, and it grieved him at his heart. (Gen. 6:5–6 KJV)

grieved
GK H6772 | S H6087 עָצַב *ʿāṣab* 14x
v. [root of: 5107, 6774, 6776, 6778, 6779, 6780; 10565]. Q to interfere with; Qp to be distressed; N to be grieved, be distressed; P to grieve; H to grieve; Ht to be filled with grief, be filled with pain.

repented
GK H5714 | S H5162 נָחַם *nāḥam* 108x
v. [root of: 4968, 5695, 5699, 5700, 5715, 5716, 5717, 5718, 5719, 5720, 9487, 9488, 9489]. N to relent, repent, change one's mind; be grieved; P to comfort, console, express sympathy; Pu to be comforted, be consoled; Ht to console oneself; to change one's mind; avenge oneself.

When I was a much younger Christian, that Scripture made me think God wished he had not made man at all. I thought he was stuck with us. That is simply not the case. God is timeless, which means he saw all of creation over all of time at the same instant. He did not make a mistake by creating us.

In both cases, the words grieved and repented are almost the same. Emotional distress about man's situation caused God great pain. Why? How can God feel pain? Isn't he in control? Can he not just snap his fingers and make things right? Isn't he all powerful and can just fix it?

Those are expected human responses. God's agape love together with his timeless existence assures that he knew *before* he created us we could not remain pure and holy. His plan to satisfy his own character of justice was always to provide *himself* as the sacrifice which met his character of mercy.

In the Garden of Gethsemane, Jesus is expressing both sides of the two-sided agape coin. He loves us, but it still grieves him as he meets his own character requirement of mercy.

Agape love is not like any other love. It is completely unselfish. Jesus isn't afraid to die. That would be easy to think from this Scripture. Not only does Jesus anticipate the crucifixion, he already fully knows the pain and suffering he will experience. Still, Jesus will *never* veer from his character. That makes him holy.

God cannot sin, which is why we call him holy. He grieved over the sin that set in motion all of mankind's sordid events. God is both the judge and the convicted criminal. He rightly judges us guilty and at the same time receives his own sentence of death.

That is why Jesus grieved at Gethsemane. We can be certain that he *never* contemplated pulling back from the cross. He focused on the joy of bringing us back to himself.

> [1] Therefore, since we are surrounded by so great a cloud of witnesses, let us also lay aside every weight, and sin which clings so closely, and let us run with endurance the race that is set before us, [2] looking to Jesus, the founder and perfecter of our faith, who for the joy that was set before him endured the cross, despising the shame, and is seated at the right hand of the throne of God. (Heb. 12:1–2 ESV)

Betrayal and Arrest. Perhaps out of habituated routine, or from the earlier discussions in the upper room, Judas left knowing where Jesus would go once the Last Supper was over. Why did the chief priests and the soldiers need Judas to identify Jesus?

What the chief priests needed was speed. Everybody already knew what Jesus looked like after the ruckus he made in the Temple. Perhaps all of Jerusalem would know him at first glance. Judas was the quickest way to locate Jesus because he knew his habit of praying in the garden. Jesus and the disciples may have discussed his after-dinner plans at the Last Supper. Either way, Judas knew precisely where to find him.

It was now nighttime, but as I've said, unless there was extensive cloud cover, the moon at that time of the month would be full.[3] That time of year, it does not commonly rain in Jerusalem, so it would have been partly cloudy at worst. Not only did Judas bring the chief priests but a large crowd including their own soldiers, elders, and a mob of people. Judas's kiss betrayed Jesus and stood as a witness against him.

Why was there a mob of people and who were they? These would probably have been people who profited from selling the sacrifice of animals and changing money in the Temple. Many people loved Jesus, but the ones that came that night had a score to settle.

It was from this crowd that the witnesses against Jesus will come. As they seized Jesus, his disciples fled. Yet even in their malicious hands Jesus showed them agape love. Who else would miraculously heal the ear of the chief priest's servant after Peter lops it off?

The mob first took him to Caiaphas's house, where the scribes and other elders were already waiting. There were many witnesses who came forward, but none could agree. The chief priests were desperate for the death penalty, but they had a couple of problems. They must follow Jewish law, which requires at least two or three witnesses. They wanted the death penalty. By Jewish law, death must be by stoning with the witnesses throwing the first one.

> [2] "If there is found among you, within any of your towns that the LORD your God is giving you, a man or woman who does what is evil in the sight of the LORD your God, in transgressing his covenant, [3] and has gone and served other gods and worshiped them, or the sun or the moon or any of the host of heaven, which I have forbidden, [4] and it is told you and you hear of it, then you shall inquire diligently, and if it is true and certain that such an abomination has been done in Israel, [5] then you shall bring out to your gates that man or woman who has done this evil thing, and you shall stone that man or woman to death with stones. [6] On the evidence of two witnesses or of three witnesses the one who is to die shall be put to death; a person shall not be put to death on the evidence of one witness. [7] The hand of the witnesses shall be first against

---

[3] Moonphase Calculator, Moonpage.com, Three Islands Press. https://www.moonpage.com/index.html?go=T&auto_dst=T&m=4&d=5&y=0030&hour=0&min=0&sec=0 or Quickphase, Quickphase.com. http://www.quickphase.com.

him to put him to death, and afterward the hand of all the people. So you shall purge the evil from your midst. (Deut. 17:2–7 ESV)

Michael Rydelnik expertly explains in his documentary film *My Search for Messiah* how there were two important things that would be lost before Shiloh, i.e., the Messiah, would come. Look at the Scripture in both the 2011 New International Version, the Amplified version, and the New American Standard version for deeper clarity.

> [10] The scepter will not depart from Judah,
>   nor the ruler's staff from between his feet,
>   until he to whom it belongs shall come
>   and the obedience of the nations shall be his.
>   (Gen. 49:10 NIV11)

> [10] The scepter or leadership shall not depart from Judah, nor the ruler's staff from between his feet, until Shiloh [the Messiah, the Peaceful One] comes to Whom it belongs, and to Him shall be the obedience of the people. (Gen. 49:10 AMP)

> [10] The scepter shall not depart from Judah,
>   Nor the ruler's staff from between his feet,
>   Until Shiloh comes,
>   And to him shall be the obedience of the peoples.
>   (Gen. 49:10 NAS)

He points out that there are *two* staffs or rods here; the scepter of leadership and the ruler's staff. The scepter of leadership is the tribal identity of Judah while the ruler's staff refers to the right to try capital offenses which result in the death penalty as described in Deuteronomy above.

Israel as a nation lost the ability to judge capital cases soon after AD 6 when Rome set Herod over Judea, its new Jewish province. Caiaphas thus could not condemn Jesus to death, and he had no control over the manner of the Roman death sentence which was crucifixion, not stoning. Judah lost tribal identity in AD 70 after the Temple was destroyed and the Jews scattered. Shiloh (Jesus Christ) had already come some forty years earlier.

After Jesus's arrest, things moved quickly over the next few hours. He was shuffled between the high priests, Herod, and Pilate. It was unlikely that the people who loved and followed him were part of the mob that took him that night. They will be shocked when Jesus will already be nailed fast by 9 a.m. that morning.

Many simply wanted a leader to throw off Rome, and not a savior. The justice of Roman and Jewish leaders is not the justice Jesus will bear. Israel, as a nation, will miss their Messiah, but by his death, they will actually be saved.

Trial and Verdict. I have questions about this passage of Scripture below. Just what *did* Caiaphas and the other high priests think Messiah was going to look like? Would they have accepted Jesus had he come riding on a horse dressed as a warrior for battle? Would he truly be God or just another man?

> [57] Then those who had seized Jesus led him to Caiaphas, the high priest, where the scribes and the elders had gathered. [58] And Peter was following him at a distance, as far as the courtyard of the high priest, and going inside he sat with the guards to see the end.
> [59] Now the chief priests and the whole council were seeking false testimony against Jesus that they might put him to death, [60] but they found none, though many false witnesses came forward.
> At last two came forward [61] and said, "This man said, 'I am able to destroy the temple of God, and to rebuild it in three days.'"
> [62] And the high priest stood up and said, "Have you no answer to make? What is it that these men testify against you?"
> [63] But Jesus remained silent. And the high priest said to him, "I adjure you by the living God, tell us if you are the Christ, the Son of God."
> [64] Jesus said to him, "You have said so. But I tell you, from now on you will see the Son of Man seated at the right hand of Power and coming on the clouds of heaven."
> [65] Then the high priest tore his robes and said, "He has uttered blasphemy. What further witnesses do we need? You have now heard his blasphemy. [66] What is your judgment?" They answered, "He deserves death."
> [67] Then they spit in his face and struck him. And some slapped him, [68] saying, "Prophesy to us, you Christ! Who is it that struck you?" (Matt. 26:57–68 ESV)

While I think they had an uneasy, but beneficial relationship with Rome, they would have attempted to use a warrior Messiah to overcome their conquerors. That they could not use Jesus probably fueled their brutality all the more.

Caiaphas and the chief priests judged that Jesus deserves death, though they could not execute a stoning. Prophetic Scripture about the Messiah specifically does not speak of stoning. The nailing of a live human being on the cross as the primary cause of death was not present at the time when the Torah and Psalms were written. Again, hanging on a tree referred to the display of a deceased body killed by stoning.

> [14] I am poured out like water,
>   and all my bones are out of joint;
> my heart is like wax;
>   it is melted within my breast;
> [15] my strength is dried up like a potsherd,
>   and my tongue sticks to my jaws;
>   you lay me in the dust of death.
> [16] For dogs encompass me;
>   a company of evildoers encircles me;
>   they have pierced my hands and feet—
> [17] I can count all my bones—
>   they stare and gloat over me;
> [18] they divide my garments among them,
>   and for my clothing they cast lots.
> [19] But you, O LORD, do not be far off!
>   O you my help, come quickly to my aid!
>   (Ps. 22:14–19 ESV)

[22] "And if a man has committed a crime punishable by death and he is put to death, and you hang him on a tree, [23] his body shall not remain all night on the tree, but you shall bury him the same day, for a hanged man is cursed by God. You shall not defile your land that the LORD your God is giving you for an inheritance. (Deut. 21:22–23ESV)

Jesus had stated that he was the Christ. That is confirmed when Caiaphas tore his robes. They then sent him to Pontius Pilate, the present Roman precept over Judea. They didn't care how he was put to death—they just wanted him dead. They did not foresee the prophetic, scriptural significance of the events that were then in motion.

But Pilate could not find any charge worthy of death. He tried to wash his hands of Jesus by sending him to Herod the Great after he hears he is a Galilean. This didn't result in anything. Jesus has already told both Caiaphas and Pilate that he was indeed the Son of God and King of the Jews. He said nothing to Herod, who only wants to see a miracle.

> [1] Then the whole company of them arose and brought him before Pilate.
> [2] And they began to accuse him, saying, "We found this man misleading our nation and forbidding us to give tribute to Caesar, and saying that he himself is Christ, a king."
> [3] And Pilate asked him, "Are you the King of the Jews?" And he answered him, "You have said so." [4] Then Pilate said to the chief priests and the crowds, "I find no guilt in this man." [5] But they were urgent, saying, "He stirs up the people, teaching throughout all Judea, from Galilee even to this place."
> [6] When Pilate heard this, he asked whether the man was a Galilean. [7] And when he learned that he belonged to Herod's jurisdiction, he sent him over to Herod, who was himself in Jerusalem at that time.
> [8] When Herod saw Jesus, he was very glad, for he had long desired to see him, because he had heard about him, and he was hoping to see some sign done by him. [9] So he questioned him at some length, but he made no answer.
> [10] The chief priests and the scribes stood by, vehemently accusing him. [11] And Herod with his soldiers treated him with contempt and mocked him. Then, arraying him in splendid clothing, he sent him back to Pilate. [12] And Herod and Pilate became friends with each other that very day, for before this they had been at enmity with each other.
> [13] Pilate then called together the chief priests and the rulers and the people, [14] and said to them, "You brought me this man as one who was misleading the people. And after examining him before you, behold, I did not find this man guilty of any of your charges against him. [15] Neither did Herod, for he sent him back to us. Look, nothing deserving death has been done by him. [16] I will therefore punish and release him." (Luke 23:1–16 ESV)

Why did Herod and Pilate become good friends that day? It seems both of them had a common distaste for the chief priests. I suspect that the chief priests probably regretted telling Pilate that Jesus was a Galilean.

On his second appearance in front of Pilate, he caved to the crowd's demand to kill Jesus. It is ironic that Jesus's blood *must* be on us in order for him to save us.

> [24] So when Pilate saw that he was gaining nothing, but rather that a riot was beginning, he took water and washed his hands before the crowd, saying, "I am innocent of this man's blood; see to it yourselves."

²⁵ And all the people answered, "His blood be on us and on our children!" (Matt. 27:24–25 ESV)

Crucifixion. Nothing remains but to carry out the sentence.

²⁷ Then the soldiers of the governor took Jesus into the governor's headquarters, and they gathered the whole battalion before him. ²⁸ And they stripped him and put a scarlet robe on him, ²⁹ and twisting together a crown of thorns, they put it on his head and put a reed in his right hand. And kneeling before him, they mocked him, saying, "Hail, King of the Jews!" ³⁰ And they spit on him and took the reed and struck him on the head.

³¹ And when they had mocked him, they stripped him of the robe and put his own clothes on him and led him away to crucify him. ³² As they went out, they found a man of Cyrene, Simon by name. They compelled this man to carry his cross.

³³ And when they came to a place called Golgotha (which means Place of a Skull), ³⁴ they offered him wine to drink, mixed with gall, but when he tasted it, he would not drink it. ³⁵ And when they had crucified him, they divided his garments among them by casting lots. ³⁶ Then they sat down and kept watch over him there. ³⁷ And over his head they put the charge against him, which read, "This is Jesus, the King of the Jews."

³⁸ Then two robbers were crucified with him, one on the right and one on the left. ³⁹ And those who passed by derided him, wagging their heads ⁴⁰ and saying, "You who would destroy the temple and rebuild it in three days, save yourself! If you are the Son of God, come down from the cross."

⁴¹ So also the chief priests, with the scribes and elders, mocked him, saying, ⁴² "He saved others; he cannot save himself. He is the King of Israel; let him come down now from the cross, and we will believe in him. ⁴³ He trusts in God; let God deliver him now, if he desires him. For he said, 'I am the Son of God.'" ⁴⁴ And the robbers who were crucified with him also reviled him in the same way.

⁴⁵ Now from the sixth hour there was darkness over all the land until the ninth hour. ⁴⁶ And about the ninth hour Jesus cried out with a loud voice, saying, "Eli, Eli, lema sabachthani?" that is, "My God, my God, why have you forsaken me?"

⁴⁷ And some of the bystanders, hearing it, said, "This man is calling Elijah." ⁴⁸ And one of them at once ran and took a sponge, filled it with sour wine, and put it on a reed and gave it to him to drink. ⁴⁹ But the others said, "Wait, let us see whether Elijah will come to save him."

⁵⁰ And Jesus cried out again with a loud voice and yielded up his spirit.[4]

⁵¹ And behold, the curtain of the temple was torn in two, from top to bottom. And the earth shook, and the rocks were split. ⁵² The tombs also were opened. And many bodies of the saints who had fallen asleep were

---

[4] See also John 19:30 ESV and Luke 23:46 ESV.

raised, [53] and coming out of the tombs after his resurrection they went into the holy city and appeared to many.

[54] When the centurion and those who were with him, keeping watch over Jesus, saw the earthquake and what took place, they were filled with awe and said, "Truly this was the Son of God!" (Matt. 27:27–54 ESV)

Burial. Jesus dies at around 3 p.m. Time is short because the Passover, a High Sabbath, is about three hours away. At dusk, just as the tomb is closed, all the other lambs will be sacrificed and roasted in homes throughout the land just as they were in Exodus 12.

[31] Since it was the day of Preparation, and so that the bodies would not remain on the cross on the Sabbath (for that Sabbath was a high day), the Jews asked Pilate that their legs might be broken and that they might be taken away.

[32] So the soldiers came and broke the legs of the first, and of the other who had been crucified with him. [33] But when they came to Jesus and saw that he was already dead, they did not break his legs. [34] But one of the soldiers pierced his side with a spear, and at once there came out blood and water.

[35] He who saw it has borne witness—his testimony is true, and he knows that he is telling the truth—that you also may believe. [36] For these things took place that the Scripture might be fulfilled: "Not one of his bones will be broken." [37] And again another Scripture says, "They will look on him whom they have pierced."

[38] After these things Joseph of Arimathea, who was a disciple of Jesus, but secretly for fear of the Jews, asked Pilate that he might take away the body of Jesus, and Pilate gave him permission. So he came and took away his body. [39] Nicodemus also, who earlier had come to Jesus by night, came bringing a mixture of myrrh and aloes, about seventy-five pounds in weight.

[40] So they took the body of Jesus and bound it in linen cloths with the spices, as is the burial custom of the Jews. [41] Now in the place where he was crucified there was a garden, and in the garden a new tomb in which no one had yet been laid. [42] So because of the Jewish day of Preparation, since the tomb was close at hand, they laid Jesus there. (John 19:31–42 ESV)

Three days in *Sheol* starts at dusk as 14 Nisan fades into 15 Nisan.

CHAPTER TEN

From Lamb to Lion

[26] "On the day of the firstfruits, when you offer a grain offering of new grain to the LORD at your Feast of Weeks, you shall have a holy convocation. You shall not do any ordinary work, [27] but offer a burnt offering, with a pleasing aroma to the LORD: two bulls from the herd, one ram, seven male lambs a year old; [28] also their grain offering of fine flour mixed with oil, three tenths of an ephah for each bull, two tenths for one ram, [29] a tenth for each of the seven lambs, [30] with one male goat, to make atonement for you." (Num. 28:26–30 ESV)

Saturday and Sunday, 18 Nisan 3790. On 14 Nisan, at 3 p.m. Jesus surrendered his life when he says, "It is finished." But it was not the end.

I'm absolutely convinced that Jesus hung there suffering on the cross until the Father told him to give his life up. It is by Jesus's words that life comes, and it is only by his words that he can give his life up. It sounds even macabre to think Jesus could have—would have—hung on that cross without dying until he uttered, "It is finished." Chilled even as I write this, I am persuaded by this Scripture.

[14] I am the good shepherd. I know my own and my own know me, [15] just as the Father knows me and I know the Father; and I lay down my life for the sheep.

[16] And I have other sheep that are not of this fold. I must bring them also, and they will listen to my voice. So there will be one flock, one shepherd.

[17] For this reason the Father loves me, because I lay down my life that I may take it up again. [18] No one takes it from me, but I lay it down of my own accord. I have authority to lay it down, and I have authority to take

it up again. This charge I have received from my Father." (John 10:14–18 ESV)

The power that Jesus had at his disposal was without measure. He told the disciples that he could command all the angels to his side at his arrest in the garden. Just as he declared the sacrifice finished and gave up his spirit, he always had the ability to take it up again. But God, the Son of Man, is obedient to God, the Father.

Jesus cannot violate his perichoretic love by disobedience. Further, all three persons of God *agree* with the plan! Such bravery is unprecedented on the behalf of so many. So why, with all his power, does Jesus wait for three days to rise again? It is part of the plan.

There would be no doubt of his death if his lifeless body were in the tomb for three days. Humans cannot go longer than about three days without water and survive, so there can be no serious claim of a hoax. Historically, three days has significant meaning in multiple places in the Bible. In Exodus, the Israelites were to travel three days into the desert to sacrifice to the Lord. There are many other examples, but it follows God's patterns.

Passover was treated just like a weekly Sabbath, but it was in fact considered a High Sabbath. The weekly Sabbath begins at dusk on Friday and ends at dusk on Saturday. Jesus was in the tomb by dusk on Wednesday and was raised at sunset on Saturday as 17 Nisan faded into 18 Nisan. That is precisely three days.

Why does no one notice until Sunday morning? There are two very good reasons. The first is obvious. Few people would have been out and no one would work on Saturday because it is Sabbath. Sunset would bring the darkness. The disciples and other men who followed Jesus were not expecting Jesus to be raised. No one was. Even the women who made the discovery were not going there expecting it.

Jesus did not need the stone removed to let him out. He had left the tomb some twelve hours earlier. Mary and Martha find the open tomb and meet a young "man" in white garb who tells them that Jesus has risen. The guards had vanished. The young man in white is there not only to give them that message, but to make sure the tomb was open so they can get inside. Mary and Martha will be the first witnesses of the grave cloth and no body.

The second reason is not so obvious. Sunday is the first day of the week, but the Sunday after Passover begins the Feast of Weeks. While Passover can vary on which day it occurs from year to year, the Feast of Weeks always begins on Sunday—the first day of the week.

Deuteronomy also suggests to me that 18 Nisan is the Feast of Firstfruits, the first day of the Feast of Weeks. As you can see, it immediately follows the description of the Passover.

> [6] But at the place that the LORD your God will choose, to make his name dwell in it, there you shall offer the Passover sacrifice, in the evening at sunset, at the time you came out of Egypt. [7] And you shall cook it and eat it at the place that the LORD your God will choose. And in the morning you shall turn and go to your tents. [8] For six days you shall eat unleavened bread, and on the seventh day there shall be a solemn assembly to the LORD your God. You shall do no work on it.
> [9] "You shall count seven weeks. Begin to count the seven weeks from the time the sickle is first put to the standing grain.
> [10] Then you shall keep the Feast of Weeks to the LORD your God with the tribute of a freewill offering from your hand, which you shall give as the LORD your God blesses you.
> [11] And you shall rejoice before the LORD your God, you and your son and your daughter, your male servant and your female servant, the Levite who is within your towns, the sojourner, the fatherless, and the widow who are among you, at the place that the LORD your God will choose, to make his name dwell there.[1] (Deut. 16:6–11 ESV)

The Feast of the Firstfruits was the first day of the Feast of Weeks when the sickle was first put to the fields for the spring harvest. People would have been busy in the fields. They would not have been looking for Jesus. Where is Jesus that day? He has gone on to Galilee as he had already told the disciples in Mark.

---

[1] Cf. Num 28:26.

²⁷ And Jesus said to them, "You will all fall away, for it is written, 'I will strike the shepherd, and the sheep will be scattered.' ²⁸ But after I am raised up, I will go before you to Galilee." (Mark 14:27 ESV)

Pentecost, which means "fiftieth," occurred the day after the Feast of Weeks ended, also on a Sunday. It is why Jesus's believers were all in one place. Jesus had already ascended to heaven ten days prior.

¹ In the first book, O Theophilus, I have dealt with all that Jesus began to do and teach, ² until the day when he was taken up, after he had given commands through the Holy Spirit to the apostles whom he had chosen. ³ He presented himself alive to them after his suffering by many proofs, appearing to them during forty days and speaking about the kingdom of God. (Acts 1:1–3 ESV)

So what happened during those three days when Jesus was dead? We don't know precisely, but we do know that Jesus was in paradise and the one thief was with him according to his own words. Where is paradise? I think paradise is Abraham's bosom on the peaceful side of the great chasm. In Jesus's account, that gulf separated Lazarus and the rich man. I think this is where that great cloud of witnesses resides whom Jesus loved too.

There were many dead raised from the grave at Jesus's death as evidence of who Jesus was. They will, like Lazarus in Bethany, have to die again. Only when the dead are finally raised incorruptible is the Scripture fulfilled. *Nissuin* is coming!

⁵⁴ When the perishable puts on the imperishable, and the mortal puts on immortality, then shall come to pass the saying that is written:
"Death is swallowed up in victory."
⁵⁵ "O death, where is your victory?
O death, where is your sting?"
⁵⁶ The sting of death is sin, and the power of sin is the law. ⁵⁷ But thanks be to God, who gives us the victory through our Lord Jesus Christ. (1 Cor. 15:54–57 ESV)

⁂

Between Justice and Mercy. Let me summarize what I've already detailed.

Jesus was nailed to the cross about the third Jewish hour, according to Mark 15:25. That is our 9 a.m. They arrested him in the middle of the night out of the public's eyes by the chief priests and those in the Temple whose financial gain from sacrifice had then been removed. The public will not have seen the shuffling between the Chief Priest, Pilate, and Herod that all occurred before dawn and ending with the death sentence.

The soldiers meted out Pilate's punishment with incredible cruelty far beyond the sentence of death by crucifixion. The crown of thorns, the mocking, the king's robe, the flogging, and the beatings are vicious. Two others are crucified on either side of Jesus, whose cross carries the notice "King of the Jews." These things have all been prophesied in Scripture and then dutifully recorded in the Gospels.

Matthew records that from the sixth hour, or noon, there was darkness over the land until he died at 3 p.m. There is no eclipse of any kind in Jerusalem.[2] Eclipses don't last for hours, but for a maximum of a few minutes. Wednesday, April 3 AD 30 is the day that I surmise Jesus died (see my included essay *Dating the Last Passover*).

At the very end, Jesus says two important things. The last thing he says is "It is finished." Why does he say this? He is God. He cannot die the way you or I do. We experience death because of our separation from God.

The time of his death is not without design. Joseph of Arimathea aided by Nicodemus would have just enough time to bury Jesus. They had to remove his body from the cross, wrap, carry, place and anoint it in the tomb before the start of Passover. The fading sunset when the stone rolled in the front of the tomb coincides closely with the slaughter of the Passover lambs. It also marks the beginning of three days.

---

[2] Daniele Cenni, *Solar Eclipse Calculator*, app data source: F Espenak, J Meeus, *Five Millennium Canon of Solar Eclipses: -1999 to +3000*, (NASA/TP-2006-214141). https://apps.apple.com/us/app/eclipse-calculator/id436018730.

What Jesus says just before his last statement is even more significant. He cries out, "My God, my God, why have you forsaken me?" But it is not a question. Is he crying out in desperation as though God has really forsaken him? Why did he make that statement?

There is in fact a very good reason for what he did. Early Hebrew Scripture was structured in *parashot*, or paragraphs. They delineated these by two Hebrew letters, *Peh* (פ) the open paragraph mark, and *Samekh* (ס). They arranged the Torah itself in 154 divisions to align with a three-year reading schedule. Modern Old Testaments use these divisions still. The New Testament was divided topically into sections called *kephalaia*. Modern chapter and verse divisions were not added until the thirteenth century. The verse numbering of Robert Estienne was added around AD 1551, and that is what we use today.

As for all in Jesus's time, the first lines of text identified the whole of the text which was being referenced. We see this technique used in Luke. Jesus would have looked for the starting line of Isaiah 11 to read the prophetic word about himself.

> [16] And he came to Nazareth, where he had been brought up. And as was his custom, he went to the synagogue on the Sabbath day, and he stood up to read. [17] And the scroll of the prophet Isaiah was given to him. He unrolled the scroll and found the place where it was written,
> [18] "The Spirit of the Lord is upon me,
>   because he has anointed me
>   to proclaim good news to the poor.
> He has sent me to proclaim liberty to the captives
>   and recovering of sight to the blind,
>   to set at liberty those who are oppressed,
> [19]   to proclaim the year of the Lord's favor."
> (Luke 4:16–19 ESV)

Jesus's statement, "My God, my God, why have you forsaken me?" was a reference aimed at all the chief priests. There was no other way to identify Scripture, so Jesus was not saying that God had forsaken him. How could God the Father and the God the Holy Spirit abandon him? God is omnipresent.

Jesus is pointing out Psalm 22 to the chief priests who are there watching him die. While David's troubles were in his mind when he wrote Psalm 22, that chapter isn't really about David. It is a circular prophecy about Jesus, and the chief priests understood *exactly* what Jesus meant. He was referring the Pharisees and chief priests to Psalm 22 because it shows them what they are seeing at that very moment. They know what Jesus is telling them. Scripture gives them real-time visual proof of who Jesus is.

Psalm 22 is a window into Jesus's spirit both before and after he dies. It marks the place between justice and mercy where they kiss. Isn't it interesting that Psalm 23 follows and is a description of us at the center of God's perichoretic love? Psalm 23 *is there* because of Psalm 22.

No one is forced to respond to God. He demonstrated how he feels about us. Like the prodigal son, we have one way back to him. Agape loves so much that he *will* give everyone what they want, no matter how much it grieves God.

Justice Rendered.

¶ *²⁰ For the choir director: A psalm of David, to be sung to the tune "Doe of the Dawn."*
¶ ¹ My God, my God, why have you abandoned me?
    Why are you so far away when I groan for help?
² Every day I call to you, my God, but you do not answer.
    Every night I lift my voice, but I find no relief.
³ Yet you are holy,
    enthroned on the praises of Israel.
⁴ Our ancestors trusted in you,
    and you rescued them.
⁵ They cried out to you and were saved.
    They trusted in you and were never disgraced.
⁶ But I am a worm and not a man.
    I am scorned and despised by all!
⁷ Everyone who sees me mocks me.
    They sneer and shake their heads, saying,
⁸ "Is this the one who relies on the LORD?
    Then let the LORD save him!
If the LORD loves him so much,
    let the LORD rescue him!"
⁹ Yet you brought me safely from my mother's womb

and led me to trust you at my mother's breast.
¹⁰ I was thrust into your arms at my birth.
    You have been my God from the moment I was born.
¹¹ Do not stay so far from me,
    for trouble is near,
    and no one else can help me.
¹² My enemies surround me like a herd of bulls;
    fierce bulls of Bashan have hemmed me in!
¹³ Like lions they open their jaws against me,
    roaring and tearing into their prey.
¹⁴ My life is poured out like water,
    and all my bones are out of joint.
My heart is like wax,
    melting within me.
¹⁵ My strength has dried up like sunbaked clay.
    My tongue sticks to the roof of my mouth.
    You have laid me in the dust and left me for dead.
¹⁶ My enemies surround me like a pack of dogs;
    an evil gang closes in on me.
    They have pierced my hands and feet.
¹⁷ I can count all my bones.
    My enemies stare at me and gloat.
¹⁸ They divide my garments among themselves
    and throw dice for my clothing.
¹⁹ O LORD, do not stay far away!
    You are my strength; come quickly to my aid!
²⁰ Save me from the sword;
    spare my precious life from these dogs.
²¹ Snatch me from the lion's jaws
    and from the horns of these wild oxen.
(Ps. 22:0–21 NLT-SE)

Mercy Provided.

¶ ²² I will proclaim your name to my brothers and sisters.
    I will praise you among your assembled people.
²³ Praise the LORD, all you who fear him!
    Honor him, all you descendants of Jacob!
    Show him reverence, all you descendants of Israel!
²⁴ For he has not ignored or belittled the suffering of the needy.
    He has not turned his back on them,
    but has listened to their cries for help.
²⁵ I will praise you in the great assembly.
    I will fulfill my vows in the presence of those who worship you.
²⁶ The poor will eat and be satisfied.

All who seek the LORD will praise him.
Their hearts will rejoice with everlasting joy.
²⁷ The whole earth will acknowledge the LORD and return to him.
All the families of the nations will bow down before him.
²⁸ For royal power belongs to the LORD.
He rules all the nations.
²⁹ Let the rich of the earth feast and worship.
Bow before him, all who are mortal,
all whose lives will end as dust.
³⁰ Our children will also serve him.
Future generations will hear about the wonders of the Lord.
³¹ His righteous Acts will be told to those not yet born.
They will hear about everything he has done.
(Ps. 22:22–31 NLT-SE)

Faith Rises.

¶ ⁰ *A psalm of David.*
¶ ¹ The LORD is my shepherd;
I have all that I need.
² He lets me rest in green meadows;
he leads me beside peaceful streams.
³ He renews my strength.
He guides me along right paths,
bringing honor to his name.
⁴ Even when I walk
through the darkest valley,
I will not be afraid,
for you are close beside me.
Your rod and your staff
protect and comfort me.
⁵ You prepare a feast for me
in the presence of my enemies.
You honor me by anointing my head with oil.
My cup overflows with blessings.
⁶ Surely your goodness and unfailing love will pursue me
all the days of my life,
and I will live in the house of the LORD
forever.
(Ps. 23:0–6 NLT-SE)

CHAPTER ELEVEN

Faith is Not Optional

The Son of Man.[1] A recent 2018 study, the State of Theology, asked some foundational survey questions with profound social implications.[2] These deserve some attention.

> **Statement 1. God is a perfect being and cannot make a mistake. True and strongly agree.** Only 55% of respondents strongly agreed with 57% female and 53% male. Those with only a high school diploma who held that view made up 61%. Those without a high school diploma were 51% while any degree of education beyond high school graduation made up 54–55%. Those with incomes below $25,000 and $50,000–$74,999 equally made up 53%. Those making $25,000–$34,999, $35,000–$49,000, $75,000–$99,999, and $100,000 and up made up 56–57%. The single, never married group and those in civil or domestic partnerships made up 47% and 42% respectively. Divorced or separated group was a little better at 53%. The widowed group made was the highest at 74%.

> **Statement 2. There is one true God in three persons: God the Father, God the Son, and God the Holy Spirit. True and strongly agree.** Overall, 56% of responses strongly agreed. This ranged from 46% of those 18–34 years and increased stepwise to 63% of those 65 and older.

---

[1] The name "Son of Man" is based on the great Messianic passage in Dan. 7:13. Compare Matt. 16:28; 19:28; 25:31; 26:64; Mark 14:62; Luke 22:69. Our Lord uses this term about eighty times to refer to Himself. It is His name as the representative Man, in the sense of 1 Cor. 15:45–47, as Son of David is distinctively His Jewish name, and Son of God His divine name. Our Lord constantly uses this term as implying that His mission (e.g. Matt. 11:19; Luke 19:10), His death and resurrection (e.g. Matt. 12:40; 20:18; 26:2), and His second coming (e.g. Matt. 24:37–44; Luke 12:40) transcend all Jewish limitations. See Cyrus I. Scofield, and Doris W. Rikkers, eds. *The Scofield® Study Bible Notes*, Matt. 8:20.
[2] The State of Theology, "Data Explorer," https://thestateoftheology.com/data-explorer? AGE=30&MF=14&REGION=30&EDUCATION=62&INCOME=254&MARITAL=126&ETHNICITY=2&RELTRAD=62&AT TENDANCE=254.

Statement 5. Biblical accounts of the physical (bodily) resurrection of Jesus are completely accurate. This event actually occurred. True and strongly agree. Only 47% of respondents strongly agreed in comparison to 63% the group comprising evangelicals, black protestant, mainline Christianity, and Roman Catholics. Evangelicals alone contrasted both those segments at 83%.

Statement 6. Jesus is the first and greatest being created by God. True and strongly agree. While overall 42% strongly agreed, 59% of evangelicals also did!

The responses to statements 1, 2, and 5 are interesting, but when you add the response rates of evangelicals to statement 6, a big red flag flies high. How can Jesus be a part of the Trinity and yet be a created being? The fact is that a large number of "believers" really don't know what they actually believe.

The *figura umbra* of the Exodus Passover which pointed to the actual events of the Last Passover is enough to support Jesus's claims to be God. Nevertheless, some erroneously contend that he made no such statements, even when Scripture is very clear. Despite the overwhelming textual evidence and the consistency of Scripture, Statement 6 indicates that there are many *believers* who doubt the validity of Jesus, the Son of God, and the Gospel message of his death and resurrection.

Who we say Jesus is steers us like the rudder of a ship, and there are only two directions from which to choose. If we say Jesus was a created being, we have implied that he was just a great teacher, and we have entirely missed the point of his coming. C. S. Lewis said it best in this timeless and oft-repeated quote.

> Yet (and this is the strange, significant thing) even His enemies, when they read the Gospels, do not usually get the impression of silliness and conceit. Still less do unprejudiced readers. Christ says that He is 'humble and meek' and we believe Him; not noticing that, if He were merely a man, humility and meekness are the very last characteristics we could attribute to some of His sayings.
>
> I am trying here to prevent anyone saying the really foolish thing that people often say about Him: 'I'm ready to accept Jesus as a great moral teacher, but I don't accept His claim to be God.' That is the one thing we must not say. A man who was merely a man and said the sort of things Jesus said would not be a great moral teacher. He would either be a lunatic—on a level with the man who says he is a poached egg—or else he would be the Devil of Hell. You must make your choice. Either this

man was, and is, the Son of God: or else a madman or something worse. You can shut Him up for a fool, you can spit at Him and kill Him as a demon; or you can fall at His feet and call Him Lord and God. But let us not come with any patronising nonsense about His being a great human teacher. He has not left that open to us. He did not intend to.[3]

Jesus was called the second Adam and for good reason.

[42] So is it with the resurrection of the dead. What is sown is perishable; what is raised is imperishable. [43] It is sown in dishonor; it is raised in glory. It is sown in weakness; it is raised in power. [44] It is sown a natural body; it is raised a spiritual body. If there is a natural body, there is also a spiritual body. [45] Thus it is written, "The first man Adam became a living being"; the last Adam became a life-giving spirit. [46] But it is not the spiritual that is first but the natural, and then the spiritual. [47] The first man was from the earth, a man of dust; the second man is from heaven. [48] As was the man of dust, so also are those who are of the dust, and as is the man of heaven, so also are those who are of heaven. (1 Cor. 15:42–48 ESV)

The first Adam had a body just as the last 'Adam' who is Jesus Christ. From there the difference is that Jesus Christ became a life-giving spirit. Notice that I said became, which means something happened to him that changed him from just a man to the Christ.

[5] For it was not to angels that God subjected the world to come, of which we are speaking. [6] It has been testified somewhere,
   "What is man, that you are mindful of him,
      or the son of man, that you care for him?
[7]   You made him for a little while lower than the angels;
      you have crowned him with glory and honor,
[8]   putting everything in subjection under his feet."
Now in putting everything in subjection to him, he left nothing outside his control. At present, we do not yet see everything in subjection to him. (Heb. 2:5–8 ESV)

The first Adam specifically had everything on earth placed under him. It was not that he just named all the animals. But that subjection man enjoyed was taken away from him when his disobedience separated him from God. Who then took over Adam's lordship?

---

[3] Lewis, *Problem of Pain*.

Up until Jesus Christ, Satan held the power of death. Consider these Scriptures, one from both the Old Testament and the New Testament.

> ⁴ Then Satan answered the LORD and said, "Skin for skin! All that a man has he will give for his life. ⁵ But stretch out your hand and touch his bone and his flesh, and he will curse you to your face." ⁶ And the LORD said to Satan, "Behold, he is in your hand; only spare his life." (Job 2:4–6 ESV)

> ¹⁴ Since therefore the children share in flesh and blood, he himself likewise partook of the same things, that through death he might destroy the one who has the power of death, that is, the devil. (Heb. 2:14 ESV)

It is clear that in Job's case, God's hedge around him precluded Satan from taking his life. The book of Hebrews confirms that Satan had the power of death. Prior to Jesus Christ, God's hedges prevent Satan's murderous rampage. What then happened when Jesus died and rose again? To answer that, let us look at the question of how the "son of God" differs from the "Son of God."

Genealogies in the New Testament are very important. Consider this in Luke which is Joseph's genealogy. Adam, his most remote ancestor, is called the son of God. He is not the Son of God.

> ²³ Jesus, when he began his ministry, was about thirty years of age, being the son (as was supposed) of Joseph, the son of Heli, ²⁴ the son of Matthat, the son of Levi, the son of Melchi, the son of Jannai, the son of Joseph, ²⁵ the son of Mattathias, the son of Amos, the son of Nahum, the son of Esli, the son of Naggai, ²⁶ the son of Maath, the son of Mattathias, the son of Semein, the son of Josech, the son of Joda, ²⁷ the son of Joanan, the son of Rhesa, the son of Zerubbabel, the son of Shealtiel, the son of Neri, ²⁸ the son of Melchi, the son of Addi, the son of Cosam, the son of Elmadam, the son of Er, ²⁹ the son of Joshua, the son of Eliezer, the son of Jorim, the son of Matthat, the son of Levi, ³⁰ the son of Simeon, the son of Judah, the son of Joseph, the son of Jonam, the son of Eliakim, ³¹ the son of Melea, the son of Menna, the son of Mattatha, the son of Nathan, the son of David, ³² the son of Jesse, the son of Obed, the son of Boaz, the son of Sala, the son of Nahshon, ³³ the son of Amminadab, the son of Admin, the son of Arni, the son of Hezron, the son of Perez, the son of Judah, ³⁴ the son of Jacob, the son of Isaac, the son of Abraham, the son of Terah, the son of Nahor, ³⁵ the son of Serug, the son of Reu, the son of Peleg, the son of Eber, the son of Shelah, ³⁶ the son of Cainan, the son of Arphaxad, the son of Shem, the son of Noah, the son of Lamech, ³⁷ the son of Methuselah, the son of

Enoch, the son of Jared, the son of Mahalaleel, the son of Cainan, [38] the son of Enos, the son of Seth, the son of <u>Adam, the son of God</u>. (Luke 3:23–38 ESV)

The book of Hebrews declares that Jesus is the begotten Son of God. Adam was made from dirt and the breath of life was breathed into him causing him to become a living spirit. Jesus was born of the Holy Spirit within the body of Mary *after* she and Joseph were legally married. He is not Joseph's seed, but by lineage he is both the son of Joseph (and thus Adam) and the Son of God.

The first Adam was the first of his kind. The second Adam, Jesus Christ, is the first of his kind. The book of Hebrews distinguishes very clearly the difference.

[5] For to which of the angels did God ever say,
 "You are my Son,
  today I have begotten you"?
Or again,
 "I will be to him a father,
  and he shall be to me a son"?
[6] And again, when he brings the firstborn into the world, he says,
 "Let all God's angels worship him."
[7] Of the angels he says,
 "He makes his angels winds,
  and his ministers a flame of fire."
[8] But of the Son he says,
 "Your throne, O God, is forever and ever,
  the scepter of uprightness is the scepter of your kingdom.
[9] You have loved righteousness and hated wickedness;
  therefore God, your God, has anointed you
  with the oil of gladness beyond your companions."[4]
[10] And,
 "You, Lord, laid the foundation of the earth in the beginning,
  and the heavens are the work of your hands;
[11] they will perish, but you remain;
  they will all wear out like a garment,
[12] like a robe you will roll them up,
  like a garment they will be changed.
 But you are the same,
  and your years will have no end."[5]
[13] And to which of the angels has he ever said,

[4] See also Psalm 45:6,7.
[5] See also Psalm 102:25–27.

> "Sit at my right hand
> until I make your enemies a footstool for your feet"?[6]
> (Heb. 1:5–13 ESV)

But the same faith that Job had then, and that we have now, saves us. His faith looked forward, and ours looks back at the second Adam, the Son of God. Remember that there is no "was" or "will be" with God. All our faith in him is "now" from God's perspective.

But you must remember that Jesus was born a man with our limitations. The difference is that he is the exact imprint of his Father. While he is human, he is the creator of all things. Hebrews is very clear about this.

> [1] Long ago, at many times and in many ways, God spoke to our fathers by the prophets, [2] but in these last days he has spoken to us by his Son, whom he appointed the heir of all things, through whom also he created the world. [3] He is the radiance of the glory of God and the exact imprint of his nature, and he upholds the universe by the word of his power. After making purification for sins, he sat down at the right hand of the Majesty on high, [4] having become as much superior to angels as the name he has inherited is more excellent than theirs. (Heb. 1:1–4 ESV)

These verses explicitly tell us something about Jesus Christ. Before he died, he was man and below the stature of the angels he created. After he is raised, he not only has all of his power and majesty restored, but he now has taken the keys of death from Satan. John records this in Revelation.

> [17] When I saw him, I fell at his feet as though dead. But he laid his right hand on me, saying, "Fear not, I am the first and the last, [18] and the living one. I died, and behold I am alive forevermore, and I have the keys of Death and Hades. (Rev. 1:17–18 ESV)

Faith is not Optional. Why does God require that we walk by faith believing that Jesus Christ is the Son of God? What really happened in Eden?

> [24] The LORD God said to the serpent,
> "Because you have done this,
>   cursed are you above all livestock
>   and above all beasts of the field;

---

[6] See also Psalm 110:1.

on your belly you shall go,
    and dust you shall eat
    all the days of your life.
15 I will put enmity between you and the woman,
    and between your offspring and her offspring;
<u>he shall bruise your head,</u>
    <u>and you shall bruise his heel</u>."
16 To the woman he said,
"I will surely multiply your pain in childbearing;
    in pain you shall bring forth children.
Your desire shall be contrary to your husband,
    but he shall rule over you."
17 And to Adam he said,
"Because you have listened to the voice of your wife
    and have eaten of the tree
of which I commanded you,
    'You shall not eat of it,'
  cursed is the ground because of you;
    in pain you shall eat of it all the days of your life;
18 thorns and thistles it shall bring forth for you;
    and you shall eat the plants of the field.
19 By the sweat of your face
    you shall eat bread,
till you return to the ground,
    for out of it you were taken;
for you are dust,
    and to dust you shall return."
20 The man called his wife's name Eve, because she was the mother of all living. 21 And the LORD God made for Adam and for his wife garments of skins and clothed them. 22 Then the LORD God said, "Behold, the man has become like one of us in knowing good and evil. Now, lest he reach out his hand and take also of the tree of life and eat, and live forever—" 23 therefore the LORD God sent him out from the garden of Eden to work the ground from which he was taken. 24 He drove out the man, and at the east of the garden of Eden he placed the cherubim and a flaming sword that turned every way to guard the way to the tree of life. (Gen. 3:14–24 ESV)

Only a tiny number of people developed faith because they physically saw Jesus Christ in the flesh. Everyone else starts in faithlessness, and some move on to faithfulness through life's experiences.

Would it not be nice if Jesus had stayed around in person all these years since God raised him from the dead? What if God had accompanied Adam and Eve as they walked out of the garden? Would that not have changed the world? Would not everyone have believed in God then? Would it not have prevented Cain from killing Abel? Would God have had to destroy the earth with a flood? Would we have seen the Jewish genocide in WW II? Would there be this present darkness?

Would Jesus even have had to die on the cross? Yes, he would have had to die still. I suspect there would have been far fewer who would have believed in God. Man would still break his relationship with God even if he were physically present. Faith is unnecessary when the genie is at your beck and call. Neither would it be possible if God were evil, and you were a slave instead of a son.

> [13] So now faith, hope, and love abide, these three; but the greatest of these is love. (1 Cor. 13:13 ESV)

It is clear that hope is sandwiched between faith and agape love. The order is significant. Faith brings hope. From hope bursts forth our agape love for God. Nothing is greater than God's core character of love.

I think agape is the final answer to all our "whys."

PART II

ESSAYS

How We Became the Bride of Christ

Weddings are a big deal. Even today, when I see a bride dressed in white, something stirs in me. Justice and mercy end in a wedding.

There was a wedding at Cana, and the wine ran out. Mary said to Jesus, "They have no wine." He replied, "Woman, what does this have to do with me? My hour has not yet come." She said to the servants, "Do whatever he tells you." Why this curious exchange? Why does Jesus's ministry begin at a wedding?

> [1] On the third day there was a wedding at Cana in Galilee, and the mother of Jesus was there. [2] Jesus also was invited to the wedding with his disciples.
> [3] When the wine ran out, the mother of Jesus said to him, "They have no wine." [4] And Jesus said to her, "Woman, what does this have to do with me? My hour has not yet come."
> [5] His mother said to the servants, "Do whatever he tells you."
> [6] Now there were six stone water jars there for the Jewish rites of purification, each holding twenty or thirty gallons. [7] Jesus said to the servants, "Fill the jars with water." And they filled them up to the brim.
> [8] And he said to them, "Now draw some out and take it to the master of the feast." So they took it.
> [9] When the master of the feast tasted the water now become wine, and did not know where it came from (though the servants who had drawn the water knew), the master of the feast called the bridegroom [10] and said to him, "Everyone serves the good wine first, and when people have drunk freely, then the poor wine. But you have kept the good wine until now."
> [11] This, the first of his signs, Jesus did at Cana in Galilee, and manifested his glory. And his disciples believed in him.
> (John 2:1–11 ESV)

Why did Jesus respond to his mother about his ministry when she was obviously interested in the lack of wine at the wedding? Why does Jesus use the wedding, and the water, and the wine to make that announcement?

I think we find the key in how ancient Jewish weddings are analogous to Jesus's relation to his church.

Ancient Jewish Weddings. Jewish weddings were contractual and both morally and religiously so recognized by the families of the bridegroom (called the *chatan*) and the bride (called the *kallah*). This contract involved the local synagogue.

The bridegroom or his father or representative (as with Isaac in Genesis 24:1–4) would initially approach the father of the woman he wished to marry. The conversation centered on the legal and practical matters attached to a potential marriage union.

Taking a bride meant transferring her economic benefit from her father's house to that of her husband. While certainly there were some tangible things that the bride would bring with her, there was not a dowry. The bridegroom or his father had to reimburse the bride's father for the economic loss of his daughter.

One might think that the bride has no say in the arrangement. While true of many eastern cultures, it was traditional in the accounts we have in the Bible for the bride's father to consult her before consenting to the offer of marriage. While they arranged the marriage, they did so with the prospective bride's consent.

This contract addresses what would happen to the bride in the event of a divorce. The bride had to be protected. Once she was married, there would be no going back to her father's house. Divorce could relegate her to a condition of poverty or worse, unless the divorcing husband were required to provide her with economic relief.

Shiddukhin. The first part of a Jewish marriage is called the *shiddukhin*. It is a legal agreement specifying the bride's price called the *mohar*, and the amount that her husband would pay to her if he later divorced her. Both the bridegroom and the bride together in the presence of their fathers signed the written document called the *ketubah*.

There are three sealed copies. One went to each family, and the other to the synagogue.

From the point of the signing, the bridegroom and the bride are legally and religiously married. This is today what we think of as the betrothal (before the troth). This is a common example of a western wedding vow today.

> "I, Eric, take thee Andrea to be my wedded wife, to have and to hold from this day forward, for better for worse, for richer for poorer, in sickness and in health, to love and to cherish, till death us do part, according to God's holy ordinance; and thereto I plight thee my troth."

Following the signing of the *ketubah*, the bridegroom and bride are husband and wife, although they have no physical connection during the *shiddukhin*. That could typically last for one to two years but even up to seven.

The bridegroom lives in a room attached to his father's house, while the bride lives in her father's house. He has not yet paid the bride-price, and neither have he and his wife sexually consummated.

The marriage is binding from the moment they sign it. Revoking the *ketubah* requires a divorce. The bridegroom must pay the bride the amount specified by the *ketubah*. The movie *The Nativity*, about Mary and Joseph, fleshes out the social and emotional effects that divorce had.

Erusin. The *shiddukhin*, or betrothal period which lasted from one or two years and sometimes up to seven, precedes the engagement period called the *erusin*. It is then that husband and wife will first consummate their marriage. It is analogous to the western tradition of exchanging troths, or vows.

The father of the bridegroom initiated the erusin. At any moment, he could tell his son to go to his wife's father's house and consummate, where he would first pay the agreed bride-price.

Then they would enter the bedroom called the *chuppah* chamber where they have their first sexual encounter called the *chuppah*. While they are consummating, their witnesses are standing just outside the chamber door. These are analogous to bridesmaids and groomsmen who act as witnesses in modern weddings.

In the bed they spread the pure white *chuppah* cloth. The bride will lie on that cloth, and as they engage in intercourse, her hymen will tear and bleed onto it.

When the husband sees the blood, he begins rejoicing loudly so that the witnesses can hear. Outside the door, their witnesses have been waiting for his cry of delight. They immediately join in exuberant celebration with the bridegroom. His bride has been proved pure.

They present the bloodied *chuppah* cloth to his bride's parents. What seems to be a crude or even vulgar ritual provides proof of her virginity should she later be accused of infidelity. Were she found not to be a virgin, the bridegroom's only option at that point was divorce.

Like the *ketubah*, the cloth carries legal weight in the case of divorce. The one to two-year lapse between the *shiddukhin* and the *erusin* is important for the bride because that is long enough to exclude pregnancy and infidelity prior to the *ketubah* and up until the *erusin*. It demonstrated to the world that the bride was pure.

There is nothing in the *erusin* that apparently tests, or even questions the husband's faithfulness. During the *shiddukhin*, though, he still lives with his father and is building a place for he and his wife to live. After the *ketubah*, merely by showing up at the *erusin* after such a long interval of physical separation would suggest his purity and commitment to a non-pregnant bride.

Nissuin. Even after the *erusin*, the bridegroom and bride are again separated. He returns to continue preparing their living quarters. She remains in her father's house. Once again, the next step, the *nissuin*, is completely in the bridegroom's father's control.

It is only at his command that his son returns for the last time. This time the bride leaves her father's house forever. They publicly celebrate the nissuin wedding feast at the *bridegroom's father's house*.

The feast declares that the marriage of husband and wife is complete. Legally, religiously, and socially established, they will live together in the household dwelling built by the husband to raise a family.

Scriptural Significance of Ancient Jewish Wedding. Modern Jewish weddings have altered and merged the *erusin* and *nissuin* to include a representation of the *chuppah* cloth which is draped on poles over the bridegroom and bride. Western tradition has reversed the whole process. Here we first have the wedding ceremony and celebration (*nissuin*), then the signing of the marriage license (*ketubah*), followed by the initial sexual encounter of the wedding night (*chuppah*).

Few today know and understand the scriptural significance associated with the original Jewish wedding process. The miracle of changing the water to wine in Cana is very significant and points to the Last Supper. The mere presence of Jesus at a wedding at the beginning of his ministry is intentional and thus also highly significant.

The events at the Cana wedding occur after Jesus's baptism in the Jordan by John the Baptist. While John recognizes he is the one who needs to be baptized, Jesus responds curiously. Here are the parallel accounts.

> [29] The next day he saw Jesus coming toward him, and said, "Behold, the Lamb of God, who takes away the sin of the world! [30] This is he of whom I said, 'After me comes a man who ranks before me, because he was before me.' [31] I myself did not know him, but for this purpose I came baptizing with water, that he might be revealed to Israel."
> (John 1:29–31 ESV)

¹³ Then Jesus came from Galilee to the Jordan to John, to be baptized by him. ¹⁴ John would have prevented him, saying, "I need to be baptized by you, and do you come to me?"
¹⁵ But Jesus answered him, "Let it be so now, for thus it is fitting for us to fulfill all righteousness." Then he consented.
¹⁶ And when Jesus was baptized, immediately he went up from the water, and behold, the heavens were opened to him, and he saw the Spirit of God descending like a dove and coming to rest on him; ¹⁷ and behold, a voice from heaven said, "This is my beloved Son, with whom I am well pleased."
(Matt. 3:13–17 ESV)

Why did Jesus need to be baptized in the first place? I suspect this represents the *mikvah*, a ceremonial washing that occurred before both the *shiddukhin* and the *erusin*. *Mikvah* was a pervasive Jewish ceremony as evidenced by *mikvah* baths throughout Israel today.

The Cana wedding miracle follows God, the father's verbal affirmation of Jesus at his baptism. Jesus is showing us that his relationship to the church, yet to be born, will be analogous to a wedding. I suggest that the Jordan baptism and the miracle at Cana are equivalent to the *ketubah*.

The Day of Preparation of Passover is always 14 Nisan. This is the day of the Last Supper. But the Last Supper is *not* a Passover meal. The sharing of bread and wine were center stage. Nothing suggests roast lamb is present as required.

Jesus does a curious thing initially. He washes all the disciples' feet first. This clearly is a ceremonial *mikvah*. One thing *mikvah* is not, is a washing to remove dirt and grime.

Next, he breaks the bread which is unleavened. Because this is the Day of Preparation of Passover, all the preparations for the Passover feast must be ready before dusk ushers it in on 15 Nisan. There was *no* leaven in the house at all as the food was prepared. Leavened bread was a daily staple, and this practice ensured that no leaven inadvertently got into the Passover meal.

The breaking and sharing of the bread represents Jesus paying the bride-price true to the order in ancient Jewish weddings. He then shares wine with them. This is analogous to the bloodied *chuppah* cloth.

> [22] And as they were eating, he took bread, and after blessing it broke it and gave it to them, and said, "Take; this is my body." [23] And he took a cup, and when he had given thanks, he gave it to them, and they all drank of it.
> [24] And he said to them, "This is my blood of the covenant which is poured out for many. [25] Truly, I say to you, I will not drink again of the fruit of the vine until that day when I drink it new in the kingdom of God." (Mark 14:22–25 ESV)

> [14] And when the hour came, he reclined at table, and the apostles with him. [15] And he said to them, "I have earnestly desired to eat this Passover with you before I suffer. [16] For I tell you I will not eat it until it is fulfilled in the kingdom of God."
> [17] And he took a cup, and when he had given thanks he said, "Take this, and divide it among yourselves. [18] For I tell you that from now on I will not drink of the fruit of the vine until the kingdom of God comes."
> [19] And he took bread, and when he had given thanks, he broke it and gave it to them, saying, "This is my body, which is given for you. Do this in remembrance of me." [20] And likewise the cup after they had eaten, saying, "This cup that is poured out for you is the new covenant in my blood…" (Luke 22:14–20 ESV)

Jesus will pay the bride-price by giving his own body on the cross symbolized by the breaking of bread. The church, his believers, are not innocent. We carry the sinfulness of our heritage. Because we cannot provide a bloodied *chuppah* cloth, Jesus does it for us by shedding his own blood on the cross. The wine symbolizes his blood.

This was so hard when Jesus made the statement to the crowd, that it caused many to stop following him. Now it is clear just how important it was. It refers specifically to the communion of the Last Supper. For me personally, taking communion is *always* a tangible act of faith that I cherish dearly.

> [53] So Jesus said to them, "Truly, truly, I say to you, unless you eat the flesh of the Son of Man and drink his blood, you have no life in you. [54] Whoever feeds on my flesh and drinks my blood has eternal life, and I will raise him up on the last day. [55] For my flesh is true food, and my blood is true drink. [56] Whoever feeds on my flesh and drinks my blood abides in me, and I in him. (John 6:53–56 ESV)

Dating the Last Passover

The Last Passover is more significant than I ever understood. The details of the last week hold many key points lost in the culture and viewpoint during Jesus's time on earth. This is the *erusin*—the second part of the ancient Jewish wedding ceremony. Believers eagerly await the call to join Jesus at the *nissuin* for that final wedding feast. Putting a date on the Last Passover and the very date of Jesus's death is highly significant. His death and resurrection were real, and dates matter.

Learning the true *day* of Jesus's death is also especially significant because it confirms to us the accuracy of scriptural prophecy and the absolute authority of Jesus's own words. We know that it happened on a Wednesday, the *day* of 14 Nisan as opposed to the *evening* of 14 Nisan.

Can we possibly determine the actual *date* of his death? I think we might. The best that I can surmise is that Jesus died on Wednesday, April 3 AD 30.

I first used a Macintosh application called *Jewish Calendar*, version 2.1.3. I created the table below using that version. The newest version, 3.1.2, however, refuses to convert Gregorian and Hebrew dates as far back as the time of the Crucifixion.

However, at this writing, this website, https://keisan.casio.com/exec/system/ 1346139486, and a newer Macintosh (and iPad and iPhone) app called

Moadim[1] both *do* calculate and convert the Gregorian and Hebrew dates. I've confirmed that it produces the same information below. *Moadim* was a free download at this writing available for Macintosh, iPad, and Window so that anyone can confirm the dates.

There are a couple of things that you need to know about dates this far back which were pointed out to me by the developer of *Jewish Calendar*.

Avi Drissman continued the app which was originally developed by Frank Yellin who he refers to in his email below. Frank Yellin has since taken back the further development of his *Jewish Calendar,* and I suspect he limited the dates it would produce. The current version does not calculate my dates anymore.

I asked Drissman who was the developer at the time, about the Passover dates in the times of the temple. When I first wrote and explained to Avi what I was trying to do with the app, he seemed less than pleased that my purpose was to figure out the date of Christ's death. I assumed him to be Jewish, and perhaps he was a bit defensive, however I did not assume that to be so.

I emailed Drissman asking the following. His comments are paraphrased. Below that are salient points about his email which need to be addressed.

> *8/22/2018*
> *Email from Ron Smith, MD to Avi Drissman*
>
> Avi, can you guide me to the methodology used by the two references for how you calculated corresponding Hebrew dates with the Gregorian calendar?
> Nothing out there can do dates as far back as the times of the last temple which is what I was using it for?
> I am a FileMaker Pro database developer since 1985 so I think I can probably develop something that would do what your app does.
> Ron Smith, MD
> Storybook Pediatrics

---

[1] *Moadim,* Safisoft.

8/22/2018
Avi's paraphrased response:

He was astonished that I was using his app (originally developed by Frank Yellin) to explore times of the last temple. Neither he nor Frank had ever put limits to prevent it returning results that far back. (It now will not calculate that far back.)

He stated several reasons he felt that the app would give nonsense results. First, Gregorian dates came into use in 1582, and he didn't think the app would properly calculate.

Second, the Hebrew dates in the time of the temple were hand adjusted. There were no fixed cycles for the days of the month. Hebrew months started when the new moon was sighted.

Before the diaspora (before AD 70), a single leader group could do this, but afterwards they were spread out.

Sometime after the diaspora, it was decided to move to a fixed formula independent of leadership.

Regular intercalation then occurred in the 2nd and 3rd centuries long after the Temple had been destroyed. As far as he knew there were no records to reconstruct their original Hebrew calendar.

The first reason he gave was about the Gregorian calendar. While it was created in 1582, one most certainly can convert prior Julian dates to Gregorian. No one indicates whether dates used before then were Julian or Gregorian. The average person assumes they are Gregorian. Avi didn't seem to support that assertion well, in my opinion.

His next point though is quite important. While we can convert dates prior to 1582 to Gregorian quite easily, there could be some issues with the hand-adjustment of the leap years for the Hebrew lunisolar calendar.

It does seem possible that even though the regular application of the leap year intercalation began as early as the second century AD, the 2nd century is still within 170 years of the AD 30. The Hebrew dates therefore *could* still be correct. Avi really does not know that they are not.

His comments, biased or not, leave some doubt about the actual date of Jesus's death, but it also cannot deny their possible validity. Perhaps future historical evidence will become available to guide us.

Beyond past Passover dates themselves, we need to establish both the best date for Jesus's birth and his age when he started his ministry. I draw your attention to the underlined text of Luke 3:1 and Luke 3:23.

[1] In the fifteenth year of the reign of Tiberius Caesar, Pontius Pilate being governor of Judea, and Herod being tetrarch of Galilee, and his brother Philip tetrarch of the region of Ituraea and Trachonitis, and Lysanias tetrarch of Abilene, [2] during the high priesthood of Annas and Caiaphas, the word of God came to John the son of Zechariah in the wilderness.

[3] And he went into all the region around the Jordan, proclaiming a baptism of repentance for the forgiveness of sins. [4] As it is written in the book of the words of Isaiah the prophet,

"The voice of one crying in the wilderness:
'Prepare the way of the Lord,
    make his paths straight.
[5] Every valley shall be filled,
    and every mountain and hill shall be made low,
and the crooked shall become straight,
    and the rough places shall become level ways,
[6] and all flesh shall see the salvation of God.'"

[7] He said therefore to the crowds that came out to be baptized by him, "You brood of vipers! Who warned you to flee from the wrath to come? [8] Bear fruits in keeping with repentance. And do not begin to say to yourselves, 'We have Abraham as our father.' For I tell you, God is able from these stones to raise up children for Abraham. [9] Even now the axe is laid to the root of the trees. Every tree therefore that does not bear good fruit is cut down and thrown into the fire."

[10] And the crowds asked him, "What then shall we do?" [11] And he answered them, "Whoever has two tunics is to share with him who has none, and whoever has food is to do likewise." [12] Tax collectors also came to be baptized and said to him, "Teacher, what shall we do?" [13] And he said to them, "Collect no more than you are authorized to do." [14] Soldiers also asked him, "And we, what shall we do?" And he said to them, "Do not extort money from anyone by threats or by false accusation, and be content with your wages."

[15] As the people were in expectation, and all were questioning in their hearts concerning John, whether he might be the Christ, [16] John answered them all, saying, "I baptize you with water, but he who is mightier than I is coming, the strap of whose sandals I am not worthy to untie. He will baptize you with the Holy Spirit and fire. [17] His winnowing fork is in his hand, to clear his threshing floor and to gather the wheat into his barn, but the chaff he will burn with unquenchable fire."

[18] So with many other exhortations he preached good news to the people. [19] But Herod the tetrarch, who had been reproved by him for

> Herodias, his brother's wife, and for all the evil things that Herod had done, [20] added this to them all, that he locked up John in prison.
> [21] Now when all the people were baptized, and when Jesus also had been baptized and was praying, the heavens were opened, [22] and the Holy Spirit descended on him in bodily form, like a dove; and a voice came from heaven, "You are my beloved Son; with you I am well pleased."
> [23] Jesus, when he began his ministry, was about thirty years of age, being the son (as was supposed) of Joseph, the son of Heli. (Luke 3:1–23 ESV)

The first verse very specifically ties the beginning of John the Baptist's ministry to the fifteenth year of the reign of Tiberius Caesar. He ruled as emperor from AD 14–37, which would mean that, at first glance, John the Baptist prepares the way of the Lord in the year AD 29.

The date of his ascension as Roman emperor in AD 14, however, does not probably correspond to his first year of reign as the verse might suggest, because of the practice of antedating where event dates were set a point earlier than previously known or recorded. While Tiberius actually ascended in AD 14 when Augustus Caesar died, he would have antedated the year of his reign from as far back to where Augustus appointed him as heir, which was AD 4. The first year of a reign also does not count the actual year of ascension usually, because the first year must be a whole, and not a partial, year. Therefore, rather than appointing Tiberius as his heir in AD 4, he probably did so in AD 1–2.[2]

The result of at least a possible error of Augustus Caesar's death, and the antedating of Tiberius Caesar's reign shifts 'the fifteenth year of his reign' from AD 29 to perhaps as early as AD 25 though it seems AD 26-27 is most likely.[3]

If AD 29 is the correct year, then there would not have been enough time for John to have been ministering and Jesus to have been baptized and start his ministry. It also would not allow time for the three documented Passovers in

---

[2] "The Chronology of Josephus," Associates for Scriptural Knowledge. http://askelm.com/star/star015.htm.
[3] Jack Finegan, *Handbook of Biblical Chronology*, 344-345.

Scripture to have occurred between Jesus's baptism and the Wednesday Preparation of Passover in AD 30.

As you can see from the table below, that particular Wednesday occurrence of Preparation of Passover of AD 30 does not occur again until AD 37 which seems far too long. Jesus would have been notably older than stated in Luke 3:23.

In conclusion, it appears to me that Jesus's ministry started circa AD 27, which is when John baptized him. This would allow for three Passovers before the Last Passover. The first Preparation of Passover was on a Wednesday, AD 25–27, with two subsequent occurrences on Monday and Saturday.

That would put the final Preparation of Passover where he was crucified on a Wednesday, 3 April AD 30 or 14 Nisan 3790.

	Day of the Week for 14 Nisan Preparation of Passover*			Age of Jesus for Variously Proposed Nativity Years†		
Hebrew Year	Gregorian / Julian		Day of Week	12 BC‡	7-5 BC§	3-2 BC‖
3770	April 14/16	10	Wed	21	14-16	11-12
3771	April 4/6	11	Mon	22	15-17	12-13
3772	Mar 23/25	12	Fri	23	16-18	13-14
3773	Apr 12/14	13	Fri	24	17-19	14-15
3774	Mar 31/Apr 2	14	Mon	25	18-20	15-16
3775	Mar 20/22	15	Fri	26	19-21	16-17
3776	Apr 8/10	16	Fri	27	20-22	17-18
3777	**Mar 29/31**	**17**	**Wed**	**28**	**21-23**	**18-19**
3778	Mar 17/19	18	Sat	29	22-24	19-20
3779	Apr 5/7	19	Fri	30	23-25	20-21
3780	**Mar 25/27**	**20**	**Wed**	**31**	**24-26**	**21-22**
3781	Apr 12/14	21	Mon	32	25-27	22-23
3782	Apr 2/4	22	Sat	33	26-28	23-24
3783	**Mar 22/24**	**23**	**Wed**	**34**	**27-29**	**24-25**
3784	**Apr 10/12**	**24**	**Wed**	**35**	**28-30**	**25-26**
3785	Mar 31/Apr 2	25	Mon	36	29-31	26-27
3786	Mar 20/26	26	Fri	37	30-32	27-28
3787	**Apr 7/9**	**27**	**Wed**	**38**	**31-33**	**28-29**
3788	Mar 27/29	28	Mon	39	32-34	29-30
3789	Apr 14/16	29	Sat	40	33-35	30-31
3790	**Apr 3/5**	**30**	**Wed**	**41**	**34-36**	**31-32**
3791	Mar 24/26	31	Mon	42	35-37	32-33
3792	Apr 12/14	32	Mon	43	36-38	33-34
3793	Apr 1/3	33	Fri	44	37-39	34-35
3794	Mar 20/22	34	Mon	45	38-40	35-36
3795	Apr 9/11	35	Mon	46	39-41	36-37
3796	Mar 28/30	36	Fri	47	40-42	37-38
3797	**Mar 18/20**	**37**	**Wed**	**48**	**41-43**	**38-39**
3798	Apr 5/7	38	Mon	49	42-44	39-40
3799	Mar 25/27	39	Fri	50	43-45	40-41
3800	Apr 13/15	40	Fri	51	44-46	41-42

*The Shepherd's Page. "Calendar Stats" [Online]. Available here http://www.abdicate.net/cal.aspx [2020.Sept.].

† Ray Summers and Jerry Vardaman. Chronos, Kairos, Christos Two. Mercer University Press, 1998, p.61-63.

‡ Vardman & Kokkinos,, Cited in Ray Summers and Jerry Vardaman, *Chronos, Kairos, Christos Two*: (Macon, Georgia: Mercer University Press, 1998), p.61-63. p.61-63.

§ Finegan & Maier, Cited in Ray Summers and Jerry Vardaman, *Chronos, Kairos, Christos Two*: (Macon, Georgia: Mercer University Press, 1998), p.61-63.

‖ Hudson, Robert. The Christian Writer's Manual of Style: 4th Edition (p. 377). Zondervan. Kindle Edition. Filmer & Martin,, Cited in Ray Summers and Jerry Vardaman, *Chronos, Kairos, Christos Two*: (Macon, Georgia: Mercer University Press, 1998), p.61-63.

Table 1. Proposed Date of the Last Passover.

Eternal or Timeless

Eternity and timelessness are not the same. While the general conception of eternity actually means timelessness, saying God is eternal is not correct. Eternity began when God created time, because he exists outside of time and cannot be confined by it.

The idea of timelessness is not a recent idea. C. S. Lewis spoke about it in the series of radio pieces that eventually became *Mere Christianity*.

> God is not hurried along in the Time-stream of this universe any more than an author is hurried along in the imaginary time of his own novel. He has infinite attention to spare for each one of us. He does not have to deal with us in the mass. You are as much alone with Him as if you were the only being He had ever created. When Christ died, He died for you individually just as much as if you had been the only man in the world.
>
> The way in which my illustration breaks down is this. In it the author gets out of one Time-series (that of the novel) only by going into another Time-series (the real one). But God, I believe, does not live in a Time-series at all. His life is not dribbled out moment by moment like ours: with Him it is, so to speak, still 1920 and already 1960. For His life is Himself.
>
> If you picture Time as a straight line along which we have to travel, then you must picture God as the whole page on which the line is drawn. "We come to the parts of the line one by one: we have to leave A behind before we get to B, and cannot reach C until we leave B behind. God, from above or outside or all round, contains the whole line, and sees it all."

He understood why God has to be timeless as you can hear in his own words. Timelessness is, however, not just a theological concept. *If timelessness exists, then there must be a timeless God.* The math for timelessness is actually quite spectacular and not really that complex, and it proves that it exists.

With Einstein's original publication of the special theory of relativity in 1905, the formula **E=mc²** was born. The concept of time dilation is a key foundation of the theory. Simply stated, it says that to every object in motion, the speed of light is the same. It is an absolute constant. For an object in motion, *time* must change since the speed of light cannot. This is extremely counterintuitive because relatively slow speeds (even of rockets and spaceships) show *almost* negligible time differences compared to stationary objects.

The faster that an object moves, the slower time passes. The classic thought experiment is of twins, one who remains on Earth while the other rockets to a far distant star at some speed ever so much closer to the speed of light.

Upon the return from his astronautical trek, the adventurer will have seemingly remained young while his brother on Earth will have gotten much older. How much older depends only on how fast the rocket was moving. Though certainly nothing in our universe generates enough energy to move an object even close to the speed of light, time dilation profoundly affects how we understand timelessness.

The equation for time dilation proves itself important in everyday life. It is real. In order for the global time on satellites and thus all places on earth to be synchronized, each satellite has to use this equation to properly adjust its onboard computer time as it orbits at different speeds around the earth. Without that adjustment, local times would drift from location to location.

In the example below, t' is the time that passes for the earthbound twin. Let that be 10 years. The speed of light is c. The velocity of the astronaut twin rocketing to a far distant star is v and t is the time that passes for him.

As the velocity of the rocket gets closer and closer to the speed of light, the time that the astronaut experiences shrinks compared to the ten years experienced by his twin brother on earth. What is significant is that if the rocket could reach the speed of light, the astronaut would see *no* time pass. That is mathematical timelessness. Table 2 shows the time dilation equation and the results of the calculation as the astronaut's speed increases. The speed of the astronaut is shown as a percentage of the speed of light which simplifies the calculations.

Time Dilation		
$$t' = t\sqrt{1 - \frac{v^2}{c^2}}$$ $\quad$ t' :: time for astronaunt $\quad$ t :: time for brother $\quad$ v :: astronaut velocity $\quad$ c :: speed of light (or 1)		
Astronaut Traveling This Percent of c *	Astronaut's Lapsed Time	Brother's Lapsed Time
50%	8.6 years	10 years
75%	6.6 years	10 years
90%	4.4 years	10 years
99%	1.4 years	10 years
99.999 9%	5 days	10 years
99.999 999%	1.2 hours	10 years
99.999 999 999 99%	44.5 seconds	10 years
99.999 999 999 999 999 99%	0.004 seconds	10 years
100%	no time	all amounts of time
* The speed of light c is 186.246 miles per second or 299,792,458 meters per second.		

Table 2. The Relative Effect of Speed on the Passage of Time

This has highly significant implications. Consider an object traveling at 99.999 999 999 999 999 999 9% of *c*, the speed of light. With a lapsed time of 0.004

seconds for the astronaut to ten years for the brother, just *one day* for the astronaut calculates to 216,000 years that would have transpired for his brother.

What we need to understand is there are *two* different perspectives of time. There is one for the astronaut traveling at high speed and one for the brother who is stationary. From the table above, time passes as a ratio of the astronaut to his brother. From the astronaut's perspective, every 0.004 seconds means that 10 years pass for his brother. That means for every second the astronaut experiences, his brother would have experienced 2,500 years, and so on. Look at the numbers that result when the astronaut is traveling just under the speed of light.

$$\frac{0.004 \; seconds \; for \; astronaut}{10 \; yrs \; for \; brother} = \frac{1 \; second \; for \; astronaut}{2,500 \; years \; for \; brother}$$

$$= \frac{1 \; day \; for \; astronaut}{216,000 \; years \; for \; brother}$$

$$= \frac{1 \; year \; for \; astronaut}{78,892,380 \; years \; for \; brother}$$

$$= \frac{6000 \; years \; for \; astronaut}{473,354,280,000 \; years \; for \; brother}$$

It is rather obvious that should the astronaut be able to experience 6000 years, that well over 473 billion years would have passed for the brother. The purported age of the universe is only between 13 and 14 billion years! Think for a moment what would happen when the astronaut's speed increased from 99.999 999 999 999 999 99% to 100% of the speed of light. At that point, time ceases to exist at all, and the astronaut would experience no time. From his perspective, the earthbound brother's time passes *all at once*!

It is also significant to understand objects shrink as they travel faster and faster toward the speed of light. At the speed of light, those objects cease to have *any* material dimension. They, and the astronaut, would just vanish.

Like that astronaut traveling at the speed of light, God is timeless. He experiences no such thing as a *before* or *after*. That's why, given the limits of our understanding of what it means, God calls himself "I AM." All times for him are the same. The mere fact that we cannot see him supports that he is indeed timeless.

Shakespeare who was outside of his stories *could* write himself into them and meet Hamlet. He would be both in *and* outside of the story, while Hamlet may only be inside. God's material presence as Jesus Christ *is* the way he wrote himself into man's story. Lewis realized this and penned the following thoughts.

> Really, a young Atheist cannot guard his faith too carefully. Dangers lie in wait for him on every side. You must not do, you must not even try to do, the will of the Father, unless you are prepared to "know of the doctrine." All my acts, desires, and thoughts were to be brought into harmony with universal Spirit. For the first time I examined myself with a seriously practical purpose. And there I found what appalled me; a zoo of lusts, a bedlam of ambitions, a nursery of fears, a harem of fondled hatreds. My name was legion.
>
> Of course, I could do nothing—I could not last out one hour—without continual conscious recourse to what I called Spirit. But the fine, philosophical distinction between this and what ordinary people call "prayer to God" breaks down as soon as you start doing it in earnest. Idealism can be talked, and even felt; it cannot be lived. It became patently absurd to go on thinking of "Spirit" as either ignorant of, or passive to, my approaches. Even if my own philosophy were true, how could the initiative lie on my side? "My own analogy, as I now first perceived, suggested the opposite: if Shakespeare and Hamlet could ever meet, it must be Shakespeare's doing. Hamlet could initiate nothing. Perhaps, even now, my Absolute Spirit still differed in some way from the God of religion. The real issue was not, or not yet, there. The real terror was that if you seriously believed in even such a "God" or "Spirit" as I admitted, a wholly new situation developed. As the dry bones shook and came together in that dreadful valley of Ezekiel's, so now a philosophical theorem, cerebrally entertained, began to stir and heave and throw off its graveclothes, and stood upright and became a living presence. I was to be allowed to play at philosophy no longer. It might, as I say, still be true that my "Spirit" differed in some way from "the God of popular religion." My Adversary waived the point. It sank into utter unimportance. He would not argue about it. He only said, "I am the Lord"; "I am that I am"; "I AM."[1]

---

[1] C. S. Lewis, *Surpised by Joy.*

Another analogy of how a timeless God interacts with those who are bound in time came to me from the movie *Miss Potter*. Mr. Norman is explaining to Miss Potter how the printing process works and why her book of illustrations, *The Tale of Peter Rabbit*, is best designed to fill no more than thirty-two pages.

The printer starts with a signature sheet upon which the book is printed, front and back, with all its pages. Some pages are upside down and so trying to read the book from the signature page itself is difficult.

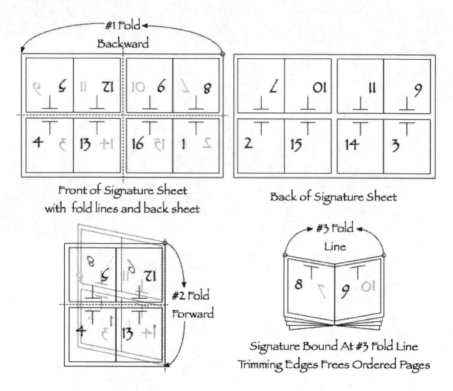

Front of Signature Sheet
with fold lines and back sheet

Back of Signature Sheet

Signature Bound At #3 Fold Line
Trimming Edges Frees Ordered Pages

It is when the signature is folded as shown, and the edges trimmed, that the book appears with all individual pages ordered and upright.

Our lives are a signature page. God creates, folds, and trims it, but we write the story one page at a time. For us, time is analogous to writing and turning the pages of our life. But a timeless God sees everything as though we have already penned the whole thing.

The Mathematics of God

What would God be if we could reduce him to our human level? That is what evolutionists attempt to do. Every opinion can be subject to bias. Mathematics is, however, objective and unbiased.

Over the course of my thirty-six-year pediatric career, I've dealt with more than a few clinical highlights and rare conditions. Two siblings come to mind who had a very rare genetic condition called CH50 disease. This disorder results from an abnormal genetic code for complement which prevents its production. Complement is the most important part of our immune system. While antibodies capture infective agents, it is complement that actually pierces the bacterial cell wall or viral capsid covering like a drill. It is the infection-killing molecule.

Most people know about antibodies, but they don't understand that antibodies don't kill bacteria and viruses. They simply mark the biologic intruders. It is complement that kills by boring a hole through the bacterial membrane or wall or the viral capsid. Those with complement deficiency (CH50 disease) cannot fight infection.

There are various defects of the complement gene which all produce the same inability to kill infectious agents. The particular defect that is found in my two sibling patients is extremely rare. In one international genome database, their genetic error was present in only three of 1,304 individuals with complement disease.

Complement deficiency, however, accounts for less than 1% of all immune deficiency diseases. The variant that these children have may be one in 2.5 million people.

Sickle cell anemia is another genetic disorder, but it is not rare at all. In 2017, there were 3.132 million people with the disease. Like CH50 disease, both mother and father must have a copy of the bad gene. Disease occurs when their child has two bad copies, one from each parent.

With CH50 disease, there is no working complement. With sickle cell disease, there is abnormal hemoglobin that makes the red blood cells change from a normal biconcave shape, to a sickle shape from which it is named. Defective red blood cells get hung in the small capillaries instead of sliding right through.

The defect in CH50 disease is a complicated and varied mix of gene abnormalities. Sickle cell disease however results when only *one* wrong amino acid occurs in an otherwise normal hemoglobin molecule. That error comes from only *one* wrong molecule within triplet of nucleic acids in the DNA segment that codes for hemoglobin.

When I was in medical school in the late 1970s, I remember a professor telling us that all of us carry some 70 separate, lethal genes. Most of them won't affect us, because they require *two* bad copies of the gene, one from each parent.

There are, in total, more lethal genes than just 70, of course. Defective genes arise over the decades as errors accumulate from generation to generation. The very first DNA (in Adam) *must* be completely correct, with all subsequent errors arising and accumulating as the population grew over hundreds and hundreds of years. These fatal genetic errors are likely part of why 10–20% of pregnancies end in spontaneous abortion.

All genetic illness results from a change in the DNA, and its sensitivity to change is extraordinary. Change is always much more likely to be detrimental than good. As a whole, there is a steady deterioration in the quality of man's DNA over time. Such change is erroneously hailed by evolutionists as the way all life today progressed from a single-celled organism. That is just not the case.

It is one thing to talk about theoretical changes, but another when you apply mathematics and statistics to it.

The basic premise is that somehow amino acids arose from heated pools of ground water puddles. They somehow aggregated into the proteins necessary for a cell to not only live, but to reproduce.

There is a chicken-egg dilemma, though. Proteins arise in all biologic organisms from the master map of the amino acid order coded in DNA. DNA maps are all read by proteins created when polymerase reads the map. But polymerase *is* itself a protein. So the question is, which came first, the DNA or the protein?

No organisms today create previously unseen de novo DNA. No proteins arise de novo and then become new DNA code. Biologic evolution theory, from the start, requires faith in a process that is not based in science.

What if somehow the DNA and the polymerase did come into complementary being in a single cell? What are the mathematical-statistical odds of getting the DNA right all in one fell swoop? The sensitivity of DNA to error produces myriad diseases far beyond CH50 disease and sickle cell disease, so the precise sequence of DNA nucleic acids *must* be completely correct before evolution could even begin. Change is almost always bad.

Change in DNA is not the same as phenotypical manifestation. Phenotype is what we can see such as the tint of skin and color of eyes and hair. All animals can adapt to their environments by expressing genetic coding differently. This is not a degradation of DNA, but a difference in gene expression that is *already* present.

There is a simple one-celled pond amoeba that could fit the bill for such an evolutionary ancestor as proposed by evolutionists. This one has 670 billion nucleic acids in its DNA sequence, probably the longest in nature. There are other amoebas with shorter DNAs, of course, but we must consider this one a worst-case scenario occurrence if we are to consider them, anyway.

Human DNA is also only around 2.9 to 3.2 billion base pairs long, but evolutionary theory suggests then that we must have shed a majority of evolutionary *unnecessary* DNA as we evolved from that first one-celled organisms. That is where our calculations must begin.

Let us start by looking at the probabilities of a simple coin flip. If you flipped three quarters *at the same time*, the odds of all being heads or all being tails is one out of eight or 0.125. The odds of two tails and one head or vice versa with no particular order required of the coins is three out of eight or 0.375.

First Quarter	Second Quarter	Third Quarter	Results
T	T	T	All tails
H	H	H	All heads
T	H	H	One tail, two heads
H	T	H	One tail, two heads
H	H	T	One tail, two heads
T	T	H	One head, two tails
T	H	T	One head, two tails
H	T	T	One head, two tails

For each quarter, if order does not matter, then there are two possibilities (heads or tails *in no particular order*) so that you have all heads, all tails, two tails and one head, or one tail and two heads. The chance for three heads (or three tails) is 1/8, while two heads and a tail or two tails and a head are each 3/8.

If we decided that we wanted to know what are the possibilities of having *specific quarters in a specific order* either heads or tails, then the chance would be 1/8 or 0.125 for each sequence. The equation to calculate that would be thus.

$$\frac{1}{2\ sides^{3\ coins}} = \frac{1}{2^3} = \frac{1}{8} = 0.125$$

More simply put, there are 8 unique combinations of coins.

But DNA isn't like flipping quarters all at once. Order matters because specific triplet sequences code for a specific amino acid. Proteins are made up of amino acids, which must be connected in the correct order so that the protein is not defective. Proteins are the building blocks and enzyme machinery which are the foundation for our bodies. Instead of three ordered coins, we are talking about *billions* of "coins," i.e., nucleic acid positions. The DNA/RNA triplet mapping table below demonstrates why even one miscoding error or missing DNA molecule results in a defective protein.

How DNA/RNA Triplets Map to Amino Acids in Proteins

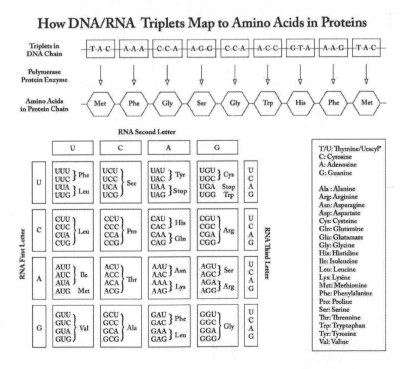

Instead of just heads or tails like a coin, each position in the DNA molecule can be 1 of 4 nucleic acids. For the amoeba, there are 670 billion nucleic acids in its DNA chain. *From the very moment it exists,* it must be absolutely correct for length and sequence in order for all cellular processes to function correctly. Otherwise everything stops and an amoeba does not exist. The odds of that happening spontaneously are 1 chance in $3.99 \times 10^{413,319,918,190}$ as shown below.[1] The length of this number is 413,319,918,191 digits!

$$4 \ nucleic \ acids \ and \ 670,000,000,000 \ DNA \ Chain =$$

$$4^{670,000,000,000} =$$

$$3.999 \times 10^{413,319,918,190} =$$

39 994 967 421 848 910 515 830 891 485 929 873 539 200
859 478 110 890 046 870 902 973 811 397 920 013 154 264
044 806 966 368 766 890 560 334 898 057 354 957 460 991
513 009 979 218 569 129 129 153 483 557 828 349 006 800
907 063 281 876 506 271 581 554 720 007 349 513 619 281
699 834 915 654 215 605 813 999 586 134 578 638 487 562
271 060 398 541 468 204 808 466 449 370 220 154 689 313
785 035 081 434 537 109 678 931 650 139 920 672 226 961
937 056 370 747 827 436 399 579 577 781 894 369 126 135
235 359 981 612 583 174 092 148 572 812 451 396 985 949
322 349 982 431 102 855 445 850 644 170 231 780 263 633
773 563 838 153 350 354 671 412 015 814 688 687 757 112
841 366 058 246 513 133 149 198 310 558 695 664 549 451
809 175 129 782 380 919 010 406 793 851 191 468 769 106
636 250 539 681 518 630 619 043 314 949 500 544 367 822
279 572 636 349 791 238 595 690 784 888 003 137 361 102
179 098 490 441 663 804 960 541 478 602 696 942 715 681
369 118 620 958 194 379 850 952 001 014 269 432 698 697
003 874 158 995 944 986 700 364 628 432 578 820 520 177
129 985 885 387 365 616 434 349 366 446 933 301 873 657
503 190 681 971 557 734 329 146 263 760 242 892 262 023
603 324 535 364 050 902 887 137 448 125 229 547 998 486
942 139 172 417 409 720 398 399 068 282 603 135 163 . . .
$\sim$ *followed by* $403,319,987,229$ *more digits* $\sim$

---

[1] This number is extremely large. I calculated it on Wolfram Alpha. You need to know also that 4^670 000 000 000 = (4^2 900 000 000)^231.This is important to know that because if you use 4^670 000 000 000 instead, Wolfram Alpha did not return a result. It did when I used (4^2 900 000 000)^231. If you go to Wolfram Alpha at https://www.wolframalpha.com you would enter that as follows: Power [Power[4,2900000000] , 231].

The enormity of this number means that there is really *no* chance that the amoeba DNA could ever occur spontaneously under any biologic conditions, no matter how extreme. Even if you try to argue that we each only carry at least 70 or more fatal genetic errors, it will not alter these odds in any meaningful way.

Mathematically, life could *not* have begun spontaneously anywhere. It had to be caused by something else greater with intention and design. Like the gears of a clock, all the sprockets must be present from the beginning, or there is no tick-tock.

The Astronomy of God

If he is timeless, then where is God? Where are we? Where is the universe? Can any space contain its creator?

I have always loved to learn. I still practiced pediatrics full time when I enrolled in a two-semester course in astronomy after twenty years of medical practice behind me. All of astronomy is fascinating to me, but when we got to inflation theory, it stunned me.

Georges Lemaître, a Belgian Catholic priest, observed in 1927 that the universe was expanding. This was confirmed by Edwin Hubble, after whom the Hubble Space Telescope was named.

The expansion could only result from a beginning and showed that the universe was much smaller at one time. In fact, Lemaître's observation meant that it had to begin its expansion from a single point called the *singularity*.

This expansion is occurring in all directions. Everything is moving away from everything else. It is much like a balloon which expands as it is inflated. All the points of space in the balloon are increasingly more distant from all the other points.

That is how the big bang theory was born. What caused the big bang, science has not and indeed cannot determine. Time and space have a beginning. What was before then and where that singularity was is a mystery to science.

The universe has a size too, as we cannot *see past* the expanding universe's edge. Because the distance across the universe is so vast, it is measured in light years. One light year is the distance that light would travel at its constant speed of 186,248.4 miles (299,792,458 meters) per second. The observable universe is 93 billion light years across, a staggering number, to be sure.[1]

This is problematic because the reported age of the universe is 13.8 billion years.[2] How can the distance across the universe be so much greater than the age of the universe? Should not the universe only be 13.8 billion light years across?

Given that we know the universe is expanding and that it all started at a single point called a singularity, it means that there was a very rapid increase in size of the universe at the beginning. In other words, the universe burst forth from a single point at time zero with all the mass that the universe has in an unimaginably small space. The temperature of that mass was unimaginably hot.

Thus *inflation theory* was born. It is postulated that, in under a second, the universe had to be suddenly inflated to a much larger size, perhaps as much as 95% of its present size. This inflation speed was much, much faster than the current expansion rate of the universe.

More importantly, the inflation of the universe occurred many, many times faster than the speed of light. But if the speed of light is always constant, and nothing can travel faster than that speed, how can the universe have expanded so fast?

This is unexplainable, unfortunately. There have been a number of theories put forth, but all have been shot through. If things move at the speed of light, they vanish according to time dilation. It creates further difficulties that often are not discussed by scientists who seek a purely material cause.

---

[1] Wolfram Alpha, https://www.wolframalpha.com/input/?i=what+is+the+distance+across+the+universe.
[2] Wolfram Alpha, https://www.wolframalpha.com/input/?i=what+is+the+age+of+the+universe.

A megaparsec is the term used for distance across a volume of space. One parsec is 3.26 light years, so a megaparsec is 3.26 billion light years distance. The expansion of the universe occurs in all directions, so every second that goes by, earth is 68 km further from objects that were 3.26 billion light years away.

It necessarily means that in the past, time has moved ever so much more slowly than at the current universe's expansion rate. The present rate of expansion is 68 km/second/megaparsec.[3] Expansion is described as the increase in size by so many kilometers per second for every megaparsec of space.

The Andromeda Galaxy is 2.573 million light years away.[4] When we calculate, that means it is moving away from Earth at over 50 kms per second! And the further it gets away from us, the faster it moves away!

This expansion affects everything we understand about earth's history. When we say that such-and-such fossil is hundreds of millions of years old, we are stating that age as though time then moved at the same rate then as it does now.

But time back then moved much, much slower, as I've discussed and demonstrated in my essay *Timelessness*. Quite simply it means that when we say the earth is 4.54 billion years old,[5] we are implying that *if* time were moving the same then as now, it would be that age.

Because of the inflation of the universe, however, I suggest that we cannot truly know the age of the earth in the terms time as we experience it. To say that a fossil is carbon dated millions of years is to then have said nothing accurate. Only recent dating outside of that intial expansion phase of the universe could carry any validity. Psalm 90 says it well when it says that a day is as a thousand years and a thousand years as a day.

---

[3] Wolfram Alpha, https://www.wolframalpha.com/input/?i=what+is+the+expansion+rate+of+the+universe.
[4] Wolfram Alpha, https://www.wolframalpha.com/input/?i=how+far+is+the+Andromeda+galaxy.
[5] Wolfram Alpha, https://www.wolframalpha.com/input/?i=how+old+is+the+earth.

³ You return man to dust
   and say, "Return, O children of man!"
⁴ For a thousand years in your sight
   are but as yesterday when it is past,
   or as a watch in the night.
⁵ You sweep them away as with a flood; they are like a dream,
   like grass that is renewed in the morning:
⁶ in the morning it flourishes and is renewed;
   in the evening it fades and withers.
   (Ps. 90:3–6 ESV)

The scientific difficulties with time are only the beginning, however. Observations of gravitational effects in the universe cannot be accounted for by its present mass. It appears that about 85% of its expected material is missing.

How can this be? Observed gravitational effects are clearly due to material mass, but if mass is missing, especially such a large amount, what is causing these effects?

This conundrum has led to many theories, most notably dark matter and dark energy. Unfortunately, we cannot see or measure dark matter or dark energy in any direct way. But if we cannot quantitate them in any way, how can they be causing such significant gravitational effects? Dark matter and dark energy probably do not exist, at least with the evidence that we presently have.

The observations are astounding. We live in a universe that initially expanded at a rate that is not possible, growing from a point that is actually nowhere into something that is actually nothing, and which has 85% less matter than expected, whose actual age in today's rate of passage of time cannot be determined.

All reference points that we use for time and space today are changing slowly and have changed drastically from the past. The further we go *back* in time, and the larger the numbers of the ages of things we discuss, the less accurate are those numbers.

That means that when we say that a fossil is 300 million years old in today's reference for time, we have no clear understanding of what 300 million years actually *is*. Argument is futile, because all our ways of measuring time are contained *within* time and thus affected by the changing rate of time versus the expansion speed of the universe.

This clearly means that when the Bible says that God created the heavens and the earth, and the earth was without form and void, that the rate of time then was so slow as to be colossal compared to our present frame of reference. Unfortunately, science has painted itself into a corner here. All these present conundrums continue to go unanswered by any but the wildest theories. Yet here we are.

In the end, the best explanation of everything remains that there is a creator. And the best explanation for why and how we could know that, is that the creator *loves* his creation. If he loves his creation, then just like our human desire is to know our children and grandchildren, we can be quite sure he wants to know us.

Our Spiritual Anatomy

While it exists for us, mercy is not extended to angels. Our spiritual anatomy reveals much about how we are different from angels who have no body. Though we are very weak compared to those spiritual brothers, he created us alone in his image.

Body. When we smell and taste delicious food, our salivary glands produce the necessary secretions to chew and begin digestion. When we hear or see something frightening, it revs up our fight-or-flight response. Sensations are the connection of our body to the physical world around us.

The animal nature of our flesh has basic needs for food, space, sexual intercourse, etc. This animal nature drives us to meet all of its needs and wants. To see the flesh in action, one only needs to watch the daily activities of a mother with a baby. Most all the needs that she meets are those of the baby's flesh.

Our flesh is the visible and physical connection that we have with time and space. It is our common link to all the other animals in the world.

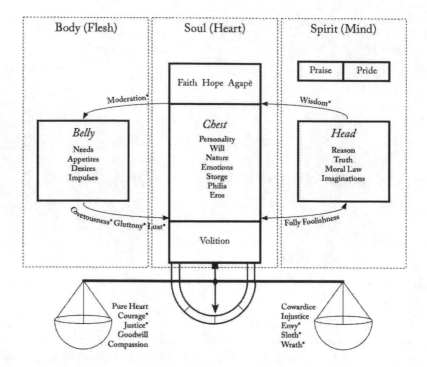

Soul. In the soul, also known as our heart, lives the personality that is our self. All that is "us" lives here in what Lewis called the chest, the seat of magnanimity or greatness. Primarily this is our will, our emotions, and the source of the three loves called *storge, philia,* and *eros.*

Storge is human love experienced by a mother nursing her baby or a father wrestling playfully in the floor with a young son. It is affectionate love.

Philia is the non-physical love between friends and is the most spiritual of the three. While *storge* usually has a biological bond or association, *philia* does not. The affection between friends is not a physical love at all, but rather a bond of mutual agreement. Friends are friends out of a mutual enjoyment of the other's company.

Eros comprises romantic love. Erotic or sexual affection is part of, though not the same as *eros.* Romantic love often begins with physical attraction, but mature *eros* grows far beyond just that.

Most importantly, all of our actions, i.e., our volitions, come through the heart before they materialize. Volition is our will expressed. All that comes out of us that is good or bad, proceeds from the act of our will. The soul is the place of our personality. It is also the seat of a depraved human nature.

Spirit. Our mind, or our spirit, is our head. It is the seat of reason, i.e., our thinking ability. It is where we keep a copy of truth, as we know it. Our reasoning ability considers everything that comes into it against our copy of the truth. The Law of Human Nature lives here too.

Our truth and the real truth may be different. We all jade our copy of truth to some extent in order to benefit ourselves. This is also part of why mankind is utterly depraved. The Law of Human Nature is like a prism through which our copy of truth passes. It compares our truth to real truth, then pokes us with our conscience. If our conscience has become worn and seared, then the pricks and pokes are just dull nudges that we learn to ignore.

Our spirit is where imagination incubates as well. These are imaginations of all things, good or bad, vain or provident.

Breath of God. How did all these parts come to be, and what will happen to them beyond the end of biologic life?

The Bible provides the account of creation which says that the animals were created before man. No doubt their physical bodies were formed from the earth just as ours. Beyond that though, God does something different. He breathed into man His own breath of life. It does not say he did the same thing with the other animals. This suggests to me that at that same point God put the spirit and soul, the mind and the heart, into us.

The very breath of God that gives us spirit and soul also breathes into us his Moral Law, The Law of Human Nature. When God finished creating, he made an amazing and very important statement. He proclaimed that everything he created was good. This was his stamp of authenticity, the mark of his very hand on mankind. At this point there was nothing spoiled in all the natural creation. Mankind contained no hint of depravity.

The Seven Deadly Sins. Dorothy Sayers is well known for her treatise on *The Other Six Deadly Sins*[1] as well as her translation and commentary on all the deadly sins in the Penguin edition of Dante's *Divine Comedy*.[2]

There are seven foundational deadly sins. Like agape love, pride is foundational. Just as all the other characteristics of God are founded on agape love, all the other deadly sins spring out of pride.

> The Seven Deadly Sins
> 1. Pride
> 2. Envy
> 3. Wrath
> 4. Sloth
> 5. Covetousness
> 6. Gluttony
> 7. Lust

Envy is the perverted desire for our own good which motivates us to deprive others of their good. The focus of envy is not simply an object. It is generalized disdain for all that is good in someone else. Covetousness and avarice, though similar, are not the same as envy. Covetousness is the pervasive desire for something that someone else has, while avarice is the love of money and power.

Wrath is a perverted love of justice that causes one to pursue spiteful revenge. God's wrath however is not a perversion because it is the settled opposition of his holy nature to all that is evil.[3] His wrath never comes out of any desire to get even. Our wrath is self-serving vengeance while his wrath is the absolute and perfect measure of perfect justice. The source of his wrath is not out of an emotional response like ours.

---

[1] Dorothy Sayers, *The Other Six Deadly Sins: An Address Given to the Public Morality Council at Caxton Hall, Westminster, on October 23rd, 1941*.

[2] Alighieri Dante, *The Divine Comedy* [in Italian] trans. by Dorothy L. Sayers.

[3] Knox Chamblin, "C. S. Lewis. - Dr. Knox Chamblin" iTunes U, 1998, https://itunes.apple.com/us/course/c.s.-lewis/id556900693.

Sloth is indifference, i.e., the failure to love any good object. It rises further than simple laziness. It is the conscious indifference to God's will. It is a man's inner voice which says to God, "Whatever!"

Gluttony, for most people, is often associated with food, but it is really far worse. It is the perverted love of pleasure. Lest we think ourselves immune from this, consider all the things that we enjoy in our life. If we have deep-seated cravings for anything that steers our actions like the rudder of a ship, then we have a perverted desire for pleasure.

Lust is the perverted love of persons. Interestingly, this is not just limited to *eros* or erotic love. Lust can also be present within *storge* and *philia*. Lewis gives a quite common example of lust within *storge* in *The Great Divorce*[4] and idolatrous lust can occur within the marriage relationship, unfortunately.[5]

Four Cardinal Virtues. There are four cardinal virtues, and they are pivotal. The original Latin word for cardinal means "the hinge of a door." Cardinal virtues have throughout time been recognized across multiple cultures and all civilized people, as well.

> The Four Cardinal Virtues
> 1. Wisdom
> 2. Moderation or Temperance
> 3. Courage
> 4. Justice or Keeping Promises

The Lord Jesus Christ's very words in Matthew 5:3–13 tell us what the hallmarks of a whole man are. This is a section of Scripture known as the Beatitudes. We tend to scan over these quickly when reading them, but we should recognize that many of these are direct opposites of the seven deadly sins. They are very important measures to size ourselves up.

> [3] "Blessed are the poor in spirit, for theirs is the kingdom of heaven.
> [4] "Blessed are those who mourn, for they shall be comforted.
> [5] "Blessed are the meek, for they shall inherit the earth.

---

[4] C. S. Lewis, *The Great Divorce.*
[5] Sheldon Vanauken, *A Severe Mercy.*

⁶ "Blessed are those who hunger and thirst for righteousness, for they shall be satisfied.
⁷ "Blessed are the merciful, for they shall receive mercy.
⁸ "Blessed are the pure in heart, for they shall see God.
⁹ "Blessed are the peacemakers, for they shall be called sons of God.
¹⁰ "Blessed are those who are persecuted for righteousness' sake, for theirs is the kingdom of heaven.
¹¹ "Blessed are you when others revile you and persecute you and utter all kinds of evil against you falsely on my account. ¹² Rejoice and be glad, for your reward is great in heaven, for so they persecuted the prophets who were before you.
¹³ "You are the salt of the earth, but if salt has lost its taste, how shall its saltiness be restored? It is no longer good for anything except to be thrown out and trampled under people's feet. (Matt. 5:3–13 ESV)

Wisdom occurs when our reason apprehends truth and then governs our will. Our heart receives wisdom, and then our volition acts accordingly. This results in courage, justice, goodwill, a pure heart, and compassion. Moderation occurs when our heart then overrules any fleshly desires or impulses.

Courage is the testing point of all the other virtues. Justice is the evidence and results of courage. Chivalry is the combination of courage and justice with the personality trait of gentleness.

How we reason is terribly important, as Proverbs 23:7 clearly states.

⁷ for he is like one who is inwardly calculating.
    "Eat and drink!" he says to you,
        but his heart is not with you.
(Prov. 23:7 ESV)

When our reason, i.e., our intellect, becomes dark or downcast, we cannot apprehend truth. Our will and volition produce cowardice, injustice, envy, sloth, or wrath. Attacks on the mind are specifically intended to darken the intellect for this very reason.⁶ The effect cascades dramatically and disastrously as 2 Corinthians 4:4 shows.

---

⁶ C. S. Lewis, *The Screwtape Letters*.

> [4] In their case the god of this world has blinded the minds of the unbelievers, to keep them from seeing the light of the gospel of the glory of Christ, who is the image of God. (2 Cor. 4:4 ESV)

Vain imaginations directly affect both truth and reason which also serves to darken the intellect as described in Romans 1:21. This darkening can affect the Heart as well.

> [1] I appeal to you therefore, brothers, by the mercies of God, to present your bodies as a living sacrifice, holy and acceptable to God, which is your spiritual worship. (ESV)

Now you might have wondered why I show volition in its own compartment. All sin that comes out of our volition leaves black marks on our soul. Once a black mark is present, we cannot erase or cover it. The process of interaction between reason, truth, and will occurs instantly and there is certainly interaction. What happens when we think bad thoughts? Do they instantly become these black marks? Mark 7:15 is quite clear here.

> [15] "There is nothing outside a person that by going into him can defile him, but the things that come out of a person are what defile him." (Mark 7:15 ESV)

Thoughts constantly flow into our reason and we instantly reference it against truth. At that moment we have the opportunity to discard it. If we don't discard it, we can deposit it into our imagination where we may revisit it, even repeatedly obsess on it time after time. If it is a vain imagination and we revisit it, we can alter our copy of truth. Folly and foolishness rather than wisdom is then injected into our will. In our heart, the vain imagination becomes an act of our volition and produces sin, a black mark on our soul.

It is critical that we actively take every thought captive as stated in 2 Corinthians 10:5. Even more though, we actively need to nurture good thoughts according to Philippians 4:8.

> [5] We destroy arguments and every lofty opinion raised against the knowledge of God, and take every thought captive to obey Christ. (2 Cor. 10:5 ESV)

⁸ Finally, brothers, whatever is true, whatever is honorable, whatever is just, whatever is pure, whatever is lovely, whatever is commendable, if there is any excellence, if there is anything worthy of praise, think about these things. (Phil. 4:8 ESV)

When reason apprehends truth, the will governs and overrules the belly. Moderation, i.e., temperance, must constantly throttle the impulses and desires of our flesh. It is important to understand that desires for food, sex, etc., have a legitimate presence in our flesh. Remember when God created man, he said it was good. He has provided a way for those desires to be met in a legitimate way, but he never intended us to be ruled by the belly.

Controlling desires of the flesh starts in the spirit. We must take every thought captive so we can moderate the flesh, otherwise covetousness, gluttony, or lust results. However, sometimes certain of these desires must be encouraged and fanned, such as in the marriage bed. A husband and a wife have a duty to encourage and nurture healthy sexual impulses toward each other, since marriage of the two is culminated in that physical connection. Paul is very clear in 1 Corinthians7:1–9.

¹ Now concerning the matters about which you wrote: "It is good for a man not to have sexual relations with a woman." ² But because of the temptation to sexual immorality, each man should have his own wife and each woman her own husband. ³ The husband should give to his wife her conjugal rights, and likewise the wife to her husband. ⁴ For the wife does not have authority over her own body, but the husband does. Likewise the husband does not have authority over his own body, but the wife does. ⁵ Do not deprive one another, except perhaps by agreement for a limited time, that you may devote yourselves to prayer; but then come together again, so that Satan may not tempt you because of your lack of self-control.
⁶ Now as a concession, not a command, I say this. ⁷ I wish that all were as I myself am. But each has his own gift from God, one of one kind and one of another.
⁸ To the unmarried and the widows I say that it is good for them to remain single, as I am. ⁹ But if they cannot exercise self-control, they should marry. For it is better to marry than to burn with passion. (1 Cor. 7:1 ESV)

All the cardinal virtues and the deadly sins have a presence within, and expression outside of us. What we say and do that results in a volitional expression of any sin leaves a black mark on our soul. It is that black mark that cannot be erased, even when the offended person has granted forgiveness. Our words echo in testimony against us forever.

But there is another black mark whose presence is not caused by any volitional act. It is the black mark of human depravity. The black marks of our individual selves prove its existence. We are utterly fallen creatures, seduced and captured by temptation in the first place. We suffer from a sinful nature which is the source of our depravity and from sin that we commit.

We could perhaps decide to continually do better until we come to a place where we can control most all the volitional sins. But what do we do about the black marks we have already accumulated? And what about the black mark of our human depravity? We can never fix that ourselves.

PART III

APPENDIX

Acknowledgments

My Bible Software. Perhaps some of you have difficulty connecting scriptural reference to the Scripture itself. Verse memorization this way is challenging for me. Scripture itself though is different. I tend to easily remember words and concepts found in passages, even though I have trouble walking to the chapter and verse associated with it.

As I've mentioned already, chapter and verse designations were not created with the Scriptures. They are a much later reference tool. Without the search capability of my software, I could be searching for hours to find a particular Scripture that comes to mind. It seems appropriate that I acknowledge what software I use. Your digital tools may be different to be sure, but any tool is probably better than nothing for studying Scripture.

In the writing of this book and for all my Bible study I used a licensed copy of *Accordance*® by Oak Tree Software. It has served me well and like a glove has a good fit. If you don't have similar software, you might want to take a look at their web site; https://www.accordancebible.com.

My Mathematics Software. It is safe to say that calculations with the size of the numbers involved in the mathematics and statistics of DNA and astronomy could not be done by the average person even twenty years ago. As computer technology advances exponentially it is also safe to assume that in the near future all my calculations will be done on personal computers, even as unimaginably large as the numbers are. To perform the calculations in this book, I used my subscription account at the Wolfram Alpha website; https://www.wolframalpha.com. They are the authors and publishers of *Mathematica®* which I also used to a degree on my desktop.

Truly accurate mathematics and statistics calculations bring an objectivity to Christian apologetics which were not possible until recent decades. If the assumptions and problems are laid out clearly and accurately, then the numbers speak without bias.

My Writing Software. In the days of my father-in-law Gilbert Morris, who authored more than a couple hundred historical fiction works, writing was done on basic word processors. For many, it is still their tool of choice. My writing tool is *Scrivener®* by Literature & Latte and can be found here; https://www.literatureandlatte.com. It is technically much more advanced that a word processor. That may be good or bad if you are considering writing yourself.

Other Software. For the Hebrew translation of *anno mundi*, I used *Mate: Universal TabTranslator* from the Apple® app store which can be found here; https://apps.apple.com/us/app/mate-universal-tab-translator/id1005088137?mt=12. The app *PopChar*™ was helpful with inserting a Hebrew font that was not coded right to left and can be found here; https://www.ergonis.com. For Hebrew dating I used *Moadim* by SafiSoft which can also be found in the app store here; https://apps.apple.com/us/app/moadim/id913651699?mt=12. Dictionary citations come from the Apple® Dictionary App, v. 2.3.0 (268), ©2005–2020 Apple Inc.

My Computer Hardware. I have been a nerdy tech person since I bought my first two Apple® Macintosh® computers in 1985. I purchased them prior to starting my solo Pediatrics practice in 1986. Over the years I have written a number of electronic billing software solutions. I deployed a full-fledge electronic medical records software in 2000, which is still the primary data management in my office. I wrote this book on a 16-inch Apple® MacBook Pro.

Bibliography

Alghieri, Dante. *The Comedy of Dante Alighieri, the Florentine: The Divine Comedy 1, 2, 3*. Translated by Dorothy L. Sayers. New York: Penguin Books, 1949.

Chamblin, Knox. *C. S. Lewis - Dr. Knox Chamblin*. Podcast. Reformed Theological Seminary, 1998. Podcast, https://itunes.apple.com/us/course/c.s.-lewis/id556900693.

Finegan, Jack. *Handbook of Biblical Chronology*. Hendrickson Pub, 1998.

Fitzmyer, Joseph A. *First Corinthians. A New Translation With Introduction and Commentary*. New Haven and London: Yale University Press, 2008.

Kohlenberger, John R., and James A. Swanson. *The Hebrew English Concordance to the Old Testament*. Zondervan, 1998.

Lewis, C. S. *Mere Christianity*. New York: Harper Collins, 2009. https://books.apple.com/us/book/mere-christianity/id360638379

Lewis, C. S. *Mere Christianity*. ePub. New York: Harper One, 2009. ePub, https://books.apple.com/us/book/mere-christianity/id360638379.

Lewis, C. S. *The Great Divorce*. ePub. New York: Harper One, 2009. ePub, https://itun.es/us/aMVFv.l.

Lewis, C. S. *The Problem of Pain*. ePub. New York: Harper One, 2009. ePub, https://books.apple.com/us/book/mere-christianity/id360638379.

Lewis, C. S. *The Screwtape Letters (Enhanced Special Edition)*. ePub. New York: Harper One, 2009. ePub, https://itun.es/us/Pckuz.l.

Lewis, C. S. *The Silver Chair*. ePub. HarperOne, 2010. ePub, https://books.apple.com/us/book/the-silver-chair/id360642541.

Lewis, C. S. *Surprised By Joy*. ePub. New York: Harper One, 2012. ePub, (presently unavailable through Apple).

Mounce, William D., and Rick D. Bennett, eds. *Mounce Concise Greek-English Dictionary of the New Testament*. Altamonte Springs, FL: Oak Tree, 2011.

Rydelnik, Michael, and Michael Vanlaningham. *The Moody Bible Commentary*. Chicago: Moody, 2014.

Rydelnik, Michael, *My Search for Messiah*. DVD. Day of Discovery, 2009.

Rydelnik, Michael, *My Search for Messiah*. DVD (2009).

Sayers, Dorothy Leigh. *The Other Six Deadly Sins, an Address Given to the Public Morality Council At Caxton Hall, Westminster on October 23rd, 1941*. London: Methuen & Co., 1943.

Scofield, Cyrus I., and Doris W. Rikkers, eds. *The Scofield® Study Bible Notes*. Oxford, England: Oxford University Press, 2003.

Smith, Ron. *A Mere Christian*. Snowy House, 2014.

Summers, Ray, and Jerry Vardaman. *Chronos, Kairos, Christos II*. Macon, Georgia: Mercer University Press, 1998.

Thompson, Francis. "The Hound of Heaven." In *The Oxford Book of English Mystical Verse*, edited by D. H. S. Nicholson, and A. H. E. Lee, Oxford: The Clarendon Press, 1917.

Qureshi, Nabeel. *Seeking Allah, Finding Jesus*. ePub. Grand Rapids, Michigan: Zondervan, 2016. ePub, https://books.apple.com/us/book/seeking-allah-finding-jesus/id667596049.

Vanauken, Sheldon. *A Severe Mercy*. ePub. New York: Harper One, 2011. ePub, https://itun.es/us/WY9tA.l.

A Guide to Kohlenberger/Mounce Hebrew-Aramaic Dictionary of the Old Testament

Throughout this book you will see references to Hebrew words from which are translated the English word we read. Translation simply refers to interpreting and translating texts written from one language into another. The Old Testament is translated from original Hebrew while the New Testament comes from Greek. Sometimes there are translations of translation. That is beyond the scope of this reference source.

Here is an example Kohlenberger/Mounce reference. The word "take" in Exodus 12:3 is translated this way in the Hebrew dictionary. Take note how it carries the sense of marriage.

> **GK H4374 | S H3947** לְקַח *lāqaḥ* 967x
> v. [root of: 4375, 4376, 4917, 4918?, 4920, 5228, 5229]. Q to take, receive; Qp to be led away; N to be captured, taken away; Pu to be taken away, brought; Ht to flash back and forth; by extension: to gain possession, exercise authority; "to take a woman" means "to marry a wife". » accept; capture; choose; deprive; get; grasp; marry; receive; seize; take.

It starts with the reference ids of the word. The first here is GK H4374. The "GK" refers to the Goodrick-Kohlenberger number. The second id is the Strong's number and is indicated by the "S." In both cases the "H" refers to the source text being Hebrew. The Strong's Dictionary also has phonetic pronunciations.

Following the reference ids is the Hebrew source word itself and the English pronunciation key. In this reference, the word לָקַח (*lāqah*, law-kakh´)is found 967 times in the Hebrew Old Testament. Next it is identified as a verb by the small "v" and other root words are given by their Kohlenberger/Mounce id number.

Following that are the various English translations for לָקַח (*lāqah*, law-kakh´) each which is preceded by a bold letter. Each bold letter indicates the translation for a particular tense of the Hebrew word. Without knowing a little about Hebrew, it is difficult to identify what tense a particular word is. Suffice it to say that the way a particular translated word is interpreted in the English we see in the Old Testament is dependent on that tense and the expertise of the translator who is doing the translation.

Because translation is dependent on the varied expertise of the translator and focus of the translation, we have the different versions of the Holy Bible. Each translator is expressing the English the way he understands it. Usually there are teams of translators so that we get the best English word from their consensus opinion. The King James Bible was originally translated by a combined group containing two subgroups of opposing scholars. This is why the King James version was a marvel of scholarly thought when it was created.

But English now is notably different from the English of King James's day. Old English is even more disparate from today's English. This is not just based on the meaning of specific words, however, but also on the varied interpretations of those words all within English speakers of the same time period.

The Living Bible was a translation to natural spoken language and was an attempt to make the Bible more accessible and understandable to the person with an average eduction. Other translations have come along since, each with a prescribed focus based on current English language use. You will find that most of the translations I use quote the English Standard Version of the Holy Bible. This does not mean that everyone has to use that version. I personally like and use it because it seems to give me a more accurate flavor of the original text. That is not always the case. Look at the difference between the Amplified and English Standard Version of the same verse in Psalms.

> ¹⁰ Mercy and loving-kindness and truth have met together; righteousness and peace have kissed each other. (Ps. 85:10 AMP)

> ¹⁰ Steadfast love and faithfulness meet; righteousness and peace kiss each other. (Ps. 85:10 ESV)

The Amplified version is where the phrase "mercy kisses justice" comes from, but the English Standard Version does not use the word "mercy" at all. Both these versions are helpful though because they increase my understanding and show how that phrase comes to be.

Though this is not intended to be a primer in any way, here is the partial list of Kohlenberger/Mounce keys showing example Hebrew verb tense comparisons[1]

Abbreviation	Full Form	Mood	Voice	Example
Q	Qal or Paal	Simple	Active	He cut
Qp	Qal passive	Simple	Passive	He is cut
N	Niphal	Simple	Passive	He was cut
P	Piel	Intensive	Active	He slashed
Pu	Paul	Intensive	Passive	He was slashed
H	Hiphil	Causative	Active	He made cut
Ho	Hophal	Causative	Passive	He was made cut
Hi	Hithpael	Intensive	Reflexive	He slashed himself

[1] Benner, Jeff A., Ancient Hebrew Reference Center, https://www.ancient-hebrew.org/roots-words/about-hebrew-nouns-and-verbs.htm

Bookmark Timeline Reference

Below is the image of the Last Passover timeline and the reference key.

The Last Passover Nisan 3790

© 2018 Ron Smith, MD. All Rights Reserved.

8 Nisan (morning), 9 Nisan (evening). Jesus Travels to Bethany to stay with Mary, Martha, and Lazarus, where he and the disciples eat with them. Jerusalem is less than two miles walk.

> A. John 12:1 Six days before the Passover, Jesus therefore came to Bethany, where Lazarus was, whom Jesus had raised from the dead.
> B. John 12:2-8 So they gave a dinner for him there. Martha served, and Lazarus was one of those reclining with him at table. Mary therefore took a pound of expensive ointment made from pure nard, and anointed the feet of Jesus and wiped his feet with her hair. The house was filled with the fragrance of the perfume. But Judas Iscariot, one of his disciples (he who was about to betray him), said, "Why was this ointment not sold for three hundred denarii and given to the poor?" He said this, not because he cared about the poor, but because he was a thief, and having charge of the moneybag he used to help himself to what was put into it. Jesus said, "Leave her alone, so that she may keep it for the day of my burial. For the poor you always have with you, but you do not always have me."

9 Nisan (morning), 10 Nisan (dusk). News of Jesus's arrival spreads and crowds come out to see both Jesus and Lazarus. The weekly Sabbath begins at dusk that Friday.

> **C. John 12:9-11** When the large crowd of the Jews learned that Jesus was there, they came, not only on account of him but also to see Lazarus, whom he had raised from the dead. So the chief priests made plans to put Lazarus to death as well, because on account of him many of the Jews were going away and believing in Jesus.

10 Nisan (morning), 10 Nisan (before dusk). Jesus rides into Jerusalem on Sabbath day as cheer him on with palm branches. Bethany is less than two miles away so traveling there does not break Jewish law. Less conspicuous is the brief visit to the empty Temple. This is nothing less than the Jesus proclaiming that the "lamb is in the House of God" fulfilling Exodus 12:3.

> **D.1 John 12:12-15** The next day the large crowd that had come to the feast heard that Jesus was coming to Jerusalem. So they took branches of palm trees and went out to meet him, crying out, "Hosanna! Blessed is he who comes in the name of the Lord, even the King of Israel!" And Jesus found a young donkey and sat on it, just as it is written, "Fear not, daughter of Zion; behold, your king is coming, sitting on a donkey's colt!"
> **D.3 John 12:23** And Jesus answered them, "The hour has come for the Son of Man to be glorified.
> **D.4 John 12:28** "Father, glorify your name." Then a voice came from heaven: "I have glorified it, and I will glorify it again."
> **D.5 Mark 11:11** And he entered Jerusalem and went into the temple. And when he had looked around at everything, as it was already late, he went out to Bethany with the twelve.

11 Nisan (morning). Jesus finds no fruit on the fig tree. The tree will never again produce fruit. He drives out those using the Temple to sell ahead of Passover. Israel is the fig tree.

> **E. Mark 11:12-16** "On the following day, when they came from Bethany, he was hungry. And seeing in the distance a fig tree in leaf, he went to see if he could find anything on it. When he came to it, he found nothing but leaves, for it was not the season for figs. And he said to it, "May no one ever eat fruit from you again." And his disciples heard it. And they came to Jerusalem. And he entered the temple and began to drive out those who sold and those who bought in the temple, and he overturned the tables of the money-changers and the seats of those who

sold pigeons. And he would not allow anyone to carry anything through the temple."

12 Nisan (morning). The angry Pharisees, without income from the merchants selling in the Temple, confront Jesus. He finds no fruit on the fig tree (Israel). The tree will never again produce fruit. He drives out those using the Temple to sell. The fig tree now withered represents their sad, spiritual state. Jesus tells of Israel and Jerusalem's fate. The Chief Priests are actively plotting to kill Jesus.

> **F1. Mark 11:20-21** As they passed by in the morning, they saw the fig tree withered away to its roots. And Peter remembered and said to him, "Rabbi, look! The fig tree that you cursed has withered."
> **F2. Mark 11:27-29** And they came again to Jerusalem. And as he was walking in the temple, the chief priests and the scribes and the elders came to him, and they said to him, "By what authority are you doing these things, or who gave you this authority to do them?" Jesus said to them, "I will ask you one question; answer me, and I will tell you by what authority I do these things. Was the baptism of John from heaven or from man? Answer me."
> **F3. Mark 13:1-2** And as he came out of the temple, one of his disciples said to him, "Look, Teacher, what wonderful stones and what wonderful buildings!" And Jesus said to him, "Do you see these great buildings? There will not be left here one stone upon another that will not be thrown down."
> **F4. Mark 13:28-29** "From the fig tree learn its lesson: as soon as its branch becomes tender and puts out its leaves, you know that summer is near. So also, when you see these things taking place, you know that he is near, eat the very gates.
> **F5. Mark 14:1-2** It was now two days before the Passover and the Feast of Unleavened Bread. And the chief priests and the scribes were seeking how to arrest him by stealth and kill him, for they said, "Not during the feast, lest there be an uproar from the people."

13 Nisan (evening). In one more day, Jesus's time comes. At Simon's house, a woman anoints him with nard, the same precious, aromatic oil used to anoint Aaron, the Ark of the Covenant, the Tent of Meeting, and all High Priests.

> **G1. Mark 14:3** And while he was at Bethany in the house of Simon the leper, as he was reclining at table, a woman came with an alabaster flask of ointment of pure nard, very costly, and she broke the flask and poured it over his head.
> **G2. Mark 14:10** Then Judas Iscariot, who was one of the twelve, went to the chief priests in order to betray him to them. And when they

heard it, they were glad and promised to give him money. And he sought an opportunity to betray him.

13 Nisan (morning). The first day of Unleavened Bread refers to the Day of Preparation, not the first feast day. Because leaven was excluded from homes on the Day of Preparation also, many Jewish communities celebrate it as the first of eight days of Feast of Unleavened Bread, instead of seven.

> **H. Mark 14:12–16** And on the first day of Unleavened Bread, when they sacrificed the Passover lamb, his disciples said to him, "Where will you have us go and prepare for you to eat the Passover?" And he sent two of his disciples and said to them, "Go into the city, and a man carrying a jar of water will meet you. Follow him, and wherever he enters, say to the master of the house, 'The Teacher says, Where is my guest room, where I may eat the Passover with my disciples?' And he will show you a large upper room furnished and ready; there prepare for us." And the disciples set out and went to the city and found it just as he had told them, and they prepared the Passover.

14 Nisan (evening). Because this is the Day of Preparation of Passover, roast lamb is not present. Rather, the Lamb of God gives a new commandment of bread and wine. The bread is the bride-price while the wine is purity of the bloodied *chuppah* cloth. This Last Supper is analogous to the *erusin* initiated by the Father of the Bridegroom after which we are forever his.

> **I1. Mark 14:17–18** And when it was evening, he came with the twelve. And as they were reclining at table and eating, Jesus said, "Truly, I say to you, one of you will betray me, one who is eating with me."
>
> **I2. Mark 14:22-24** And as they were eating, he took bread, and after blessing it broke it and gave it to them, and said, "Take; this is my body." And he took a cup, and when he had given thanks he gave it to them, and they all drank of it. And he said to them, "This is my blood of the covenant, which is poured out for many.
>
> **J1. Mark 14:26** And when they had sung a hymn, they went out to the Mount of Olives.
>
> **J2. Mark 14:32–33** And they went to a place called Gethsemane. And he said to his disciples, "Sit here while I pray." And he took with him Peter and James and John, and began to be greatly distressed and troubled.
>
> **J3. Mark 14:43** And immediately, while he was still speaking, Judas came, one of the twelve, and with him a crowd with swords and clubs, from the chief priests and the scribes and the elders.
>
> **J4. Mark 14:55** Now the chief priests and the whole council were seeking testimony against Jesus to put him to death, but they found

none. But he remained silent and made no answer. Again the high priest asked him, "Are you the Christ, the Son of the Blessed?" And Jesus said, "I am, and you will see the Son of Man seated at the right hand of Power, and coming with the clouds of heaven." And the high priest tore his garments and said,

J5. Mark 14:61–64 What further witnesses do we need? You have heard his blasphemy. What is your decision?" And they all condemned him as deserving death.

J6. Mark 14:72 And immediately the rooster crowed a second time. And Peter remembered how Jesus had said to him, "Before the rooster crows twice, you will deny me three times." And he broke down and wept.

14 Nisan (morning). Jesus is condemned, flogged, beaten, and finally nailed to the cross by the third Jewish hour (9 a.m.). By the sixth hour (3 p.m.), Jesus is dead having finished his work.

K1. Mark 15:1–2 And as soon as it was morning, the chief priests held a consultation with the elders and scribes and the whole council. And they bound Jesus and led him away and delivered him over to Pilate. And Pilate asked him, "Are you the King of the Jews?" And he answered him, "You have said so."

K2. John 19:14 Now it was the day of Preparation of the Passover. It was about the sixth hour. He said to the Jews, "Behold your King!"

K3. John 19:16–18 So he delivered him over to them to be crucified.

So they took Jesus, and he went out, bearing his own cross, to the place called The Place of a Skull, which in Aramaic is called Golgotha. There they crucified him, and with him two others, one on either side, and Jesus between them.

K4. John 19:23–27 When the soldiers had crucified Jesus, they took his garments and divided them into four parts, one part for each soldier; also his tunic. But the tunic was seamless, woven in one piece from top to bottom, so they said to one another, "Let us not tear it, but cast lots for it to see whose it shall be." This was to fulfill the Scripture which says, "They divided my garments among them, and for my clothing they cast lots."

So the soldiers did these things, but standing by the cross of Jesus were his mother and his mother's sister, Mary the wife of Clopas, and Mary Magdalene. When Jesus saw his mother and the disciple whom he loved standing nearby, he said to his mother, "Woman, behold, your son!" Then he said to the disciple, "Behold, your mother!" And from that hour the disciple took her to his own home.

14 Nisan (late afternoon) and 15 Nisan (dusk). Jesus is Jesus is removed from the cross, his body treated with spices and wrapped in linen, and he has been placed in a new grave.

> **L1. John 19:28–30** After this, Jesus, knowing that all was now finished, said (to fulfill the Scripture), "I thirst." A jar full of sour wine stood there, so they put a sponge full of the sour wine on a hyssop branch and held it to his mouth. When Jesus had received the sour wine, he said, "It is finished," and he bowed his head and gave up his spirit.
>
> **L2. Mark 15:37–39** And Jesus uttered a loud cry and breathed his last. And the curtain of the temple was torn in two, from top to bottom. And when the centurion, who stood facing him, saw that in this way he breathed his last, he said, "Truly this man was the Son of God!"
>
> **L3. Mark 15:43–45** Joseph of Arimathea, a respected member of the council, who was also himself looking for the kingdom of God, took courage and went to Pilate and asked for the body of Jesus. Pilate was surprised to hear that he should have already died. And summoning the centurion, he asked him whether he was already dead. And when he learned from the centurion that he was dead, he granted the corpse to Joseph."
>
> **L4. John 19:31–34** Since it was the day of Preparation, and so that the bodies would not remain on the cross on the Sabbath {for that Sabbath was a high day}, the Jews asked Pilate that their legs might be broken and that they might be taken away. So the soldiers came and broke the legs of the first, and of the other who had been crucified with him. But when they came to Jesus and saw that he was already dead, they did not break his legs. But one of the soldiers pierced his side with a spear, and at once there came out blood and water.
>
> **L5. Mark 15:46** And Joseph bought a linen shroud, and taking him down, wrapped him in the linen shroud and laid him in a tomb that had been cut out of the rock. And he rolled a stone against the entrance of the tomb.

18 Nisan (evening). As the weekly Sabbath wanes at dusk, Jesus rises from the dead as night falls. Most everyone is inside getting ready for bed. It is only at the first light of morning that several women find his grave empty.

> **M. Mark 16:2–7** And very early on the first day of the week, when the sun had risen, they went to the tomb. And they were saying to one another, "Who will roll away the stone for us from the entrance of the tomb?" And looking up, they saw that the stone had been rolled back—it was very large. And entering the tomb, they saw a young man sitting on the right side, dressed in a white robe, and they were alarmed. And he said to them, "Do not be alarmed. You seek Jesus of Nazareth, who was crucified. He has risen; he is not here. See the place where they laid

him. But go, tell his disciples and Peter that he is going before you to Galilee. There you will see him, just as he told you."

Our Testimony

We lived out Lewis's statement through our Laura who died in 2012. The quote below from Lewis that I shared in Chapter 1, is painfully close for Stacy and me. Laura set my life on a different course. I doubt this book would ever have been written, if not for her.

> "If God were good, He would wish to make His creatures perfectly happy, and if God were almighty, He would be able to do what He wished. But the creatures are not happy. Therefore, God lacks either goodness, or power, or both." This is the problem of pain, in its simplest form.

Every part of our life will help you understand how this book really started. When Laura died, my heart was left with all the why's. The answers started coming as I pressed into his love. I'm not seminary trained, but I take great comfort in knowing that C. S. Lewis was not either. God is very capable, but he cannot snap his fingers and instantly change things. His love puts boundaries on what he will or will not and can or cannot do.

Pain is not something God caused. We own that. In its awfulness, pain opens a crack in us where his light and love can shine. He wastes nothing to press in close, and we cannot stop him loving us no matter how we injure him. The only way pain ends is if God accepted our justice—the justice that *we* rightly earned.

He is good. He does want to make us happy. His plan is playing out to bring us back to him, and most people will not come easily. In the end he will redeem all who ask and then end their pain forever.

> 8 He will swallow up death forever;
>   and the Lord GOD will wipe away tears from all faces,
>   and the reproach of his people he will take away from all the earth,
>   for the LORD has spoken.
>   Is. 25:8 (ESV)

Laura. I just retired from general pediatrics after thirty-six years. I graduated medical school in 1983, and I started my career after residency in Oklahoma.

Stacy and I married young. She was twenty, and I was just nineteen. I started medical school at just twenty-one. Though my family was poor when I was young, my dad built his natural gas pipeline business into a three-state operation. He dropped out of school in the eighth grade, and he and mom dreamed of giving their sons the opportunities they never had.

Stacy's father, Gilbert Morris, taught English at Ouachita Baptist University in Arkadelphia where we lived. A popular and prolific historical fiction novelist, he authored well over two hundred books. He preached part-time filling in mostly where needed at small Baptist churches.

I accepted the Lord as my personal savior at the age of four. Stacy, too, came to know him when she was very young. We follow him still as we enter our sixties.

Andrea was born in 1984, while we were still in residency in Oklahoma. I brought my family back to a small Arkansas town near the Louisiana border. Laura was born there after our first year in solo practice. During Stacy's pregnancy with Laura, things took an unexpected turn.

Our little Laura was born with fetal isotretinoin embryopathy because Stacy was on a prescription medicine called Accutane. Stacy got pregnant even though we were taking double precautions. Those nine months were awful. We prayed.

She never progressed developmentally beyond three months. Stacy and I cared for her ourselves at home until she passed away at twenty-four.

By age thirteen, Laura's choking during feeding became so bad that she could only feed through a GI button in her stomach. Serious implications following the surgery to place that feeding port in her abdomen resulted in a one-month PICU stay. Four more surgeries followed before she was discharged. Stacy and I stayed by her side. I slept on the floor by her bed, and Stacy took the one convertible chair.

She recovered, but from then on the years didn't seem kind. She developed seizures. On a number of occasions, Stacy and I worked sometimes for several hours to stop them. It took large doses of anticonvulsant to get them stopped, and they occurred more frequently toward the end.

As if it weren't difficult enough being a father to a disabled child, I was also her physician. There were only about three hundred other children with her condition. Though my residence training was good, nothing could have prepared me for what we faced.

Finally, on April 24, 2012, Laura passed away with all her family all around her. A sudden brain bleed led to emergency surgery on a Friday. Though Saturday looked better, she crashed on Sunday, and by Monday we knew she was gone. On Tuesday, we handed our little Laura back to our Lord.

I have already made the case for timelessness and how it is not the same as eternity. My understanding of the difference came as Stacy and I were standing in the funeral home making final arrangements with the secretary there. As we handed over a poem—really a prayer—which was penned in my pain for Laura, God proved to us that he had heard our cries.

Laura passed away on April 24, 2012. The poem was dated April 24, 1992. I remembered back when I had written it how the Lord urged me forward. I cried out to him with the same intensity as my pain. God knew the day Laura would come to him. He had nudged me to write the poem exactly twenty years before then.

In that instant, God affirmed to Stacy and me that he had been with us all that time. How else could those two dates be exactly twenty years apart? Seasoned Christian believers that we were, and having done medical missions worldwide, we were suddenly and keenly aware of how much God loved us.

I know God is timeless. I know we are eternal. I know that he loves us and he had no part in Laura's illness. We live in a broken world of man's own making. Believing that anyone else caused our own pain is no small lie. God never intended our world to be what it is.

Christians seeking to make their life smooth, painless, and well-provisioned should stop. Though he is coming and will see to those things, remember that *he himself is the prize.* There is no substitute.

Forever And A Day For Laura Michelle, by Ron Smith, MD, April 24, 1992
...now being confident of this, that he who began a good work in you will carry it on to completion until the day of Christ Jesus.—Philippians 1:6
I started praying for a little child the other day.
  'Cause I was sure that was God's way
To heal that little one and make her whole.
  I was sure of this royal goal.
Her little body was twisted and turned.
  Oh, how in my heart the desire burned,
For her wholeness all at once to see,
  And then to be all that she could be.
As I prayed, the Holy One spoke quietly
  To my inner man on bended knee.
How long will you wait, how long will you believe
  For this miracle that in your heart I've conceived?
I thought only momentarily, and said,
  God, I'm your servant, I wait in your stead
If it be a day, a month, a year or three,
  I'll wait, I'll wait, I'll wait, this miracle to see!
Days, months, years passed by,
  And it seemed the Lord waited, I don't know why,
To heal my little girl, such a precious sight,
  So small and frail, sometimes I would just cry.

But His words to me would echo,
    And in my spirit man, I knew it would be so.
How long will I wait, how long will I believe,
    For this miracle that in my heart you've conceived?
Forever And A Day,
    That's the only way
 stand in faith, for this my child.
    Though it seems her healing hides,
        it will only be a little while.

Index

Printed in the United States
By Bookmasters